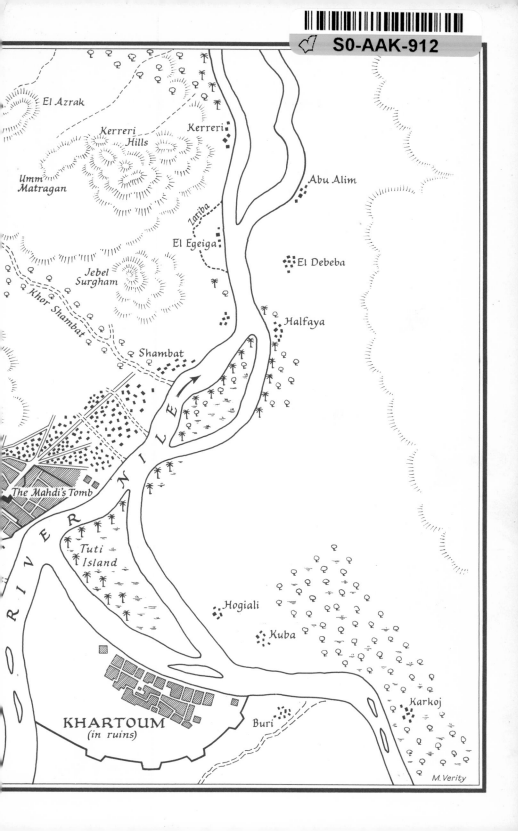

El Azrak

Kerreri
Hills

Kerreri

Umm
Matragan

Abu Alim

Zariba

El Egeiga

El Debeba

Jebel
Surgham

Khor Shambat

Halfaya

Shambat

R I V E R   N I L E

The Mahdi's Tomb

Tuti
Island

Hogiali

Kuba

Karkoj

KHARTOUM
(in ruins)

Buri

M. Verity

OMDURMAN

Philip Ziegler

OMDURMAN

ALFRED A. KNOPF

NEW YORK

1974

FOR TOBY
who contributed greatly
in his own way

THIS IS A BORZOI BOOK
PUBLISHED BY ALFRED A. KNOPF, INC.

Copyright © 1973 by Philip Ziegler

All rights reserved under International and Pan-American Copyright Conventions
Published in the United States by Alfred A. Knopf, Inc., New York
Distributed by Random House, Inc., New York
Originally published by William Collins Sons and Co. Ltd., London

Set in Monophoto Bembo
Made and printed in The Netherlands
by de Lange/van Leer NV Amsterdam & Deventer

Library of Congress Catalog Card Number: 73–8230
ISBN 0–394–48936–5

First American Edition

Contents

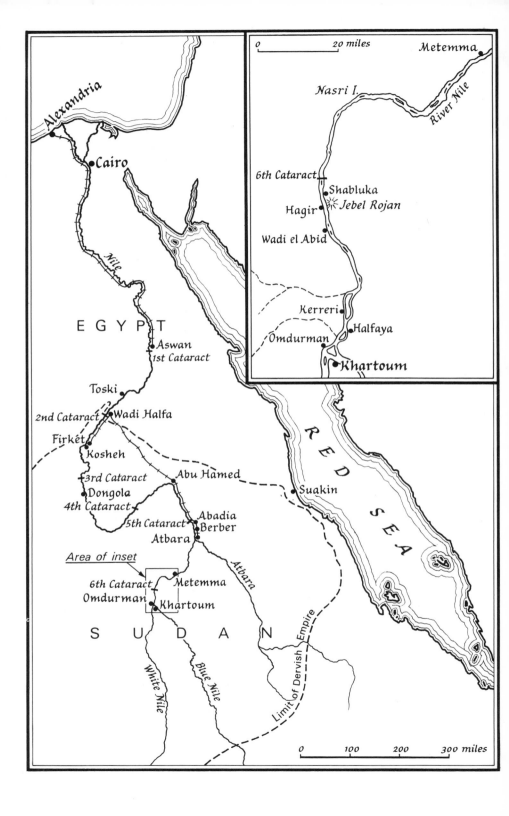

Foreword

THIS is a book about the battle of Omdurman and the few days that led up to it; seeking to bring the action to life by drawing on the many records of participants which survive in books, regimental journals and manuscript collections. It is not a book about the Sudan campaigns of 1896 to 1898 – for that the reader will still do best to turn to Winston Churchill's *The River War*. Though sometimes egocentric in approach and inaccurate in detail this is a magnificent history which reads as well today as when first written. Still less have I written a political or social study of the Sudan; for this the best recourse is P. M. Holt's excellent *The Mahdist State in the Sudan*. My intention is more modest: it is to describe the battle in such a way that the reader will know something of what it was like to be there, what it felt like to face the headlong assault of twenty thousand dervishes or to charge with the 21st Lancers into what seemed almost certain destruction. If I have succeeded it is largely thanks to those soldiers whose personal accounts, written for family and friends, speak with an authenticity which no historian can surpass.

The transliteration of Arabic is notoriously difficult. I have adopted the somewhat over-simplified solution of using the version which it seems to me will be most readily recognised by the general reader. This will hardly satisfy the scholar, but since no one scholar is likely to agree with another on what is in fact correct, the layman can perhaps be permitted to follow his own fancy. I am nevertheless most grateful to Mr Alan Goulty of the British Embassy, Khartoum, for remedying some impossibilities and inconsistencies.

Prologue

EARLY in the morning of January 26, 1885, the dervish armies stormed the ramparts of Khartoum. To the starving and demoralised garrison the final onslaught can have come as no surprise; the wonder was rather that it had been delayed so long. For more than three hundred days the rebel forces under their leader, the Mahdi, had massed around the walls of the city. Little by little the net had grown tighter, supplies of grain and ammunition had dwindled, the Egyptian and Sudanese defenders had slipped away to make peace with the new high priest and hero of Islam. Each day General Gordon climbed to the roof of his palace to scan the waters of the Nile for the smoke of the long-awaited steamers with reinforcements and supplies. Each day he saw only the leaden waters, the distant palm-fringed banks, the kites and buzzards circling attentively overhead. Far to the north the relief force, too slow in starting, too leisurely in advance, crawled uneasily towards its goal.

Still the Mahdi held his hand. Even after he had overrun the fort at Omdurman on the other side of the river and had massed all his forces against the city, he seemed curiously loath to apply the *coup de grâce*. He pleaded with Gordon to surrender, promising him honourable terms, freedom to return to England without even the payment of any ransom. Contemptuously Gordon ignored the offer; he had prepared for himself a martyr's bed and nothing was going to stop him lying in it except the total capitulation of all his adversaries – a group in which Mr Gladstone's government in London played a part almost as prominent as the dervish hordes. And then the Mahdi received the news that the vanguard of the relief expedition was within a few days of Khartoum. If Gordon's garrison were to be overrun, it had to be done at once. One restriction only was imposed on the attackers by their leader: let the infidels and 'Turks' be butchered, the women raped, the city burned and looted – the life of Gordon must be spared.

And so, at 3.30 a.m. the Ansar infantry had crept stealthily towards the moat and hurled themselves, with appalling ferocity, upon the battered walls of Khartoum. They had expected savage fighting, instead the defences crumbled before them. A few strong points held out but these were the exceptions; for the most part the garrison, weakened by hunger and lack of sleep, convinced of the inevitability of defeat, cowered before the invaders and pleaded for their lives. The plea was rarely heeded. But the massacre of the despised Egyptians did not sate the appetite of the dervishes. Now they swarmed towards the palace, cutting down the few guards who dared oppose them. The swelling cacophony of victors and vanquished warned Gordon that the moment of his martyrdom was near.

When the news of the attack had been brought him he had risen and dressed carefully in white uniform, sword and tarbush. Now he tranquilly awaited the arrival of the enemy. Even if he had known of the Mahdi's order that he should be taken alive he would have had little faith in the discipline and restraint of his assailants. As the first dervishes reached the foot of the staircase outside his quarters he stepped out to confront them, revolver in hand. 'Where is your master, the Mahdi?' Gordon cried. For an instant the bright blades rested, the clamour for blood was stilled. But one man, however fearless, cannot check a torrent. The spell snapped. 'Oh cursed one, your time is come!' and the foremost dervish hurled his heavy spear

9

full against Gordon's chest. He stumbled, fell back and his killers were upon him, hacking and stabbing at the twitching body. In a few seconds it was all over. Khartoum had fallen. Gordon was dead.

A mile or so away, Slatin Pasha, the Austrian adventurer who had become Governor of Darfur and now prisoner of the Mahdi, was lying in heavy chains awaiting the outcome of the battle. A Christian who had purchased his life by turning Moslem when captured by the dervish forces, he had thereby earned the contempt of Gordon and had been chillingly rebuffed when he sought to escape and rally to the government forces. Now, however, he knew that his fate was inextricably linked with the man who had rejected him: if Khartoum could hold out until the relief expedition arrived, then surely the Mahdi's empire would melt away and his prisoners regain their liberty?

Slatin had dropped off into a fitful doze when he was woken at dawn by the uproar. Anxiously peering into the grey half-light he awaited the outcome of what he knew must be the crucial battle for the city. Soon messengers came running with the news that Khartoum had fallen. Still Slatin prayed that the stories were exaggerated. He crawled laboriously a few yards from his tent and listened to the uproar coming from the direction of the dervish headquarters. Soon he saw members of the Mahdi's bodyguard striding towards him. One of them carried a bloody cloth wrapped carelessly about some round, lumpish object. He stopped in front of the prisoner and, with an insulting gesture, pulled away the cloth to show the contents. Slatin found himself staring at the head of Gordon: 'his blue eyes were half opened; the mouth was perfectly natural; the hair of his head and his short whiskers were almost quite white.'

Forty-eight hours later the steamers bearing the advance guard of the relief force came into sight of Khartoum.

The Mahdi

They saw the smoking ruins of Gordon's palace, and the place where his flag had flown; then turned and steamed back down the river, to bring the news to the main body of the expeditionary force at Metemma. Their retreat heralded the withdrawal of the whole Anglo–Egyptian army. England receded from the Sudan, leaving the Mahdist empire to make what it could of the vast hinterland.

Major Herbert Kitchener of the Royal Engineers, an ambitious young officer serving with the Egyptian cavalry, had been charged by the commander of the expeditionary force with the duty of keeping in touch with Gordon and reporting on the state of affairs within the beseiged city. This task he had performed as well as his limited resources permitted him.

The news of Gordon's death dismayed him, but his chagrin was as nothing to the rage and shame which he felt when it became certain that the British were to withdraw without more ado from the Sudan. The honour of the nation had been besmirched and must be washed clean. The issue, he wrote, lay between 'anarchy – a return to savagedom and great dangers to Egypt . . . or the development of an enormous trade in central Africa, under a good government.' But the danger to Egypt and the possibilities for trade were of marginal importance in his eyes. The essential was that Gordon must be avenged. This obsession with the need for vengeance never left him, rather it grew with the years. When fourteen years later he sent the army into action his order of the day concluded:

'The Sirdar is absolutely confident that every officer and man will do his duty. He only wishes to impress on them the words: "Remember Gordon". The enemy before them are Gordon's murderers.'

Through the long years between the fall of Khartoum and the final destruction of Mahdism on the field of Omdurman, Kitchener never ceased to obey his own injunction and remember Gordon. Only when he rode, triumphant, through the streets of Omdurman with Slatin Pasha at his side did he feel that Gordon's murder had at last been satisfactorily avenged.

CHAPTER I

The Years of Preparation

In telling this story it would be out of place to describe in any detail what happened between the fall of Khartoum and Kitchener's crowning victory. Some explanation, however, is needed if the scene is to be set for what was to follow.

Surveyed with the doubtful wisdom of hindsight it seems as if, from the start, it was inevitable that the British would eventually seek to reconquer the Sudan and avenge their slaughtered martyr. To contemporaries things looked very different. In a fine flurry of indignation, Queen and country reviled the prime minister, Mr Gladstone, for his failure to act more swiftly and more resolutely. Having thus made their contribution to the nation's spiritual welfare they thankfully put the matter from their minds. Gladstone was forced reluctantly to proclaim that the rule of the Mahdi must be crushed, but when he shelved the enterprise indefinitely in favour of an adventure in Afghanistan, hardly a voice was raised in protest. The public memory is notoriously short and when too energetic an exercise of the faculty is likely to involve both bloodshed and higher taxation, then it is likely that things will be forgotten almost before they have taken place. The British forgot Gordon and forgot the Sudan; they would have liked to forget Egypt as well, but here we were so inextricably involved that, with the best will in the world, total oblivion proved impossible. Though theoretically independent, Egypt was in fact little more than a colony and its 'ruler', the Khedive, ruled little beyond his palace walls.

Yet it was the state of Egypt which was later to contribute greatly to a change of heart. Under the direction of Evelyn Baring, from 1892 Lord Cromer, this former cesspit of maladministration and corruption was becoming a reasonably prosperous and well-ordered state. The news was trumpeted to the world by Alfred Milner in his *England in Egypt*, a book which did much to foster a new pride in our imperial role. Then came the death of Gladstone and, in 1895, the formation of Lord Salisbury's administration. Imperialism as a dynamic philosophy became respectable, even fashionable. Egypt, with India, was cited as an area of the world where its effects had been of unequivocal benevolence. But to the south of this ornament to the imperial crown stalked fearful anarchy. Egypt could never be safe while barbarians menaced her frontiers. Worse still, behind the barbarians lurked the French, threatening always to carve their way across northern Africa, *our* Africa, and sever us for ever from our possessions to the south.

But it was probably another book which did as much as anything to swing British opinion in favour of intervention in the Sudan. For more than ten years Slatin Pasha had been the prisoner of the Mahdi and his successor Abdullahi, the Khalifa. Sometimes he had been treated as honoured counsellor, sometimes as abject slave, but always he had felt himself degraded and dishonoured. Then, in 1895, he escaped and wrote a memoir of his captivity and of the Mahdist empire. Skilfully translated by Kitchener's future Director of Intelligence, Reginald Wingate, this majestic polemic gave reinforcement to all those who argued that an invasion of the Sudan was long overdue. It had, indeed, been written and translated with no other object. It painted a picture of a sullen, tormented land, ravaged by plague and famine; where genocide was a commonplace and political murder almost more the rule than the exception. Its despot, the Khalifa, corrupt,

Execution of Sudanese by the Mahdi

treacherous, sadistically cruel, maintained his sway by terror and was hated by all but a handful of his subjects. So black was his villainy, indeed, that it was hard to imagine how Slatin had survived his long years of captivity, let alone escaped. As with the somewhat similar recollections of another prisoner in Omdurman, Father Ohrwalder, however, the British public were in no mood to question the revelations. They accepted them as the unvarnished truth and felt appropriately outraged. If this was what went on in the Sudan, then how could decent men stand by and take no action?

Slatin's account was by no means entirely fantasy. The Khalifa *was* a cruel and cunning man. Ever since he had inherited the government of the Sudan after the death of the Mahdi in June, 1885, he had had to fight to maintain his position. Arab politics are rarely conducted with the decorum attained in certain other lands, and in the circumstances of the Sudan the squeamish and the scrupulous could not hope to survive for long. The Khalifa was neither the one nor the other. But nor was he a monster. As a young man he had above all been conspicuous for his asceticism, his courage and his dedicated loyalty to the Mahdi and the cause of Islam. He was still brave and still devoted to the Mahdi's memory, and though the asceticism had been eroded by the ministrations of cooks and concubines, he had not grown soft. He was cruel, but only by the standards of the alien; ruthless, but no more than was essential if he were to hold together his ramshackle empire. He could be generous, even tolerant; his chunky smallpox-ridden face could light up with strikingly attractive charm. He was a man whom even Slatin had found it hard to hate and impossible to despise. His chief weaknesses as a leader were inordinate vanity and a conviction that his cause was bound to triumph. Blind certainty of victory in battle can be an excellent thing when allied to superior fire power but may prove lethally expensive if indulged in from a position of great weakness.

In fact his empire was by no means the administrative disaster which Slatin depicted. Conditions were indeed unpleasant for the inhabitants, but this was to a large extent no fault of the Khalifa, for the plagues of Egypt seemed to have moved inexorably south during the period of his rule. To the traditional frogs, lice and flies or blains, hail and locusts, the last decade of the nineteenth century added drought, cholera and small red mice. Weakened by famine the debilitated dervishes died in their tens of thousands from the epidemics which ravaged the towns and villages. The Khalifa compounded the disaster by initiating mass movements of population; justifiable, perhaps, on political grounds but disastrous socially. He shifted his own people, the nomadic Taiasha, *en bloc* to the new capital at Omdurman, and deported the less amenable tribes with harsh efficiency. But accusations of genocide seem to have been unfair. He was not vindictive, and no more brutal than his needs dictated. He held together the ramshackle heritage which the Mahdi had bequeathed him and kept some semblance of order, if not of law, throughout his realm. By many he was revered as a national hero and, if there could have been a plebiscite among the more aware of the inhabitants of the Sudan, he would probably have been confirmed in office by a handsome majority.

It goes almost without saying that the Sudan under British rule was to be more prosperous and more secure than its Mahdist predecessor. Whether this provides a sufficient justification for its annexation is a question to which each generation will return a different answer. What is at least certain is that the British had no economic incentive for invading the Sudan; the conventional caricature of the greedy imperialist grabbing the raw materials of the less developed countries has no application here. All that could be expected was a protracted and costly campaign with no tangible reward at the end except the still more protracted and costly business of putting the derelict state into working order.

What in fact eventually induced the British government in 1896 to undertake the expedition was neither benevolent imperialism nor a belated lust for revenge but the needs of European politics. It was Lord Salisbury's wish to shore up the Triple Alliance and do something to please Italy and Germany which made intervention in the Sudan seem desirable.

The Italians from Eritrea had recently been routed by the Abyssinians at the battle of Adowa and there was some – though no particularly convincing – reason to suspect that the Sudanese were planning a further campaign in alliance with their southern neighbour. Some form of intervention by the Anglo–Egyptian forces on the Egyptian frontier with the Sudan might check whatever the Khalifa had in mind: even if he had nothing in mind, the

Gordon's Last Stand
Painting by G. W. Joy

British action would at least have attested to our good-will towards the Italians. At that time, at least so far as Whitehall was concerned, there was no question of continuing the advance to Khartoum or of substituting Anglo-Egyptian rule for the Khalifa's administration. But though the government might plan with prudence, the soldiers remembered that they had a score to settle with the Sudanese. British policy might be to make a brief diversionary incursion to the south: the Egyptian army was out to avenge Gordon, and the only place where Gordon could fully be avenged was the Khalifa's new capital of Omdurman.

The Egyptian army in 1896 was a very different affair from the rabble which had been dissolved by British decree some fourteen years before. 'It appeared easier to draw sunbeams out of cucumbers than to put courage into the fellah,' wrote Churchill, but first Sir Evelyn Wood and later Sir Francis Grenfell, the British commanders of the Khedive's army, applied themselves to this arduous task. Their success was striking. A score of dedicated British officers and as many N.C.O.s managed to enthuse this motley force of Egyptians and Sudanese with a fresh pride and sense of purpose. A trained and disciplined body emerged gradually from the shadows of degradation and despair. The new army had its baptism of fire at Toski in 1889 when a Mahdist invasion of Egypt was thrown back with heavy loss. The victory did wonders for the morale of the fledgeling force. Though the dervishes would not credit it, their easy triumphs were things of the past; in future they had to reckon with organised opposition which would test them to the uttermost.

In 1892 Grenfell resigned as Sirdar, or commander-in-chief, of the Egyptian army. Herbert Kitchener had commanded the cavalry at Toski, and won the respect of his commander-in-chief. His work as Adjutant-General had proved his flair for organisation. Perhaps as important, he had established firm friendships with those men whose voices were heard when new appointments were being discussed in London – above all, with the prime minister, Lord Salisbury. By the strict rules of hierarchy, however, he could not hope to succeed in Grenfell's place and in Cairo, where hierarchy was esteemed as all-important and Kitchener anyway considered a vulgar upstart, the possibility of his promotion was hardly considered. When his selection as Sirdar was announced, the reaction among the British in Cairo and their Egyptian hangers-on was one of dismay and disgust. The dismay dwindled as his undoubted competence became better realised, the disgust was never wholly to pass away.

Few major figures of the epoch can have been less prepossessing than Kitchener. This dour, lowering figure seemed unable to relax or to establish true friendship with any human being, to show feeling or to derive pleasure from any pursuit outside his chosen profession. Arrogant with his inferiors, uneasy with his peers; he was obsequious only with those who might advance his career, and even here churlishness sometimes got the better of discretion. His physical appearance – the coarse, beefy face; heavy, empurpled jowls; glazed, rolling eyes; opulent yet disciplined moustache – seemed somehow to reflect his character: strong, brutish, inflexible. 'He may be a general, but never a gentleman,' wrote Churchill to his mother, and if the word 'gentleman' be taken to assume some sensitivity to and respect for the feelings of others, then the stricture was wholly justified.

This is, of course, to see only the black side of his nature. He was courageous, hard-working, honourable, loyal to those who served him well, totally reliable. His ferocious ambition might make him hard with others but it made him harder still with himself. Whether he was personally agreeable was, anyway, irrelevant to the needs of the day.

His qualities and qualifications might have been tailor-made for the operation which he was to undertake. Imagination, quick-thinking, strategic or tactical flair were hardly to be called for at the highest level; what was needed was patience, perseverance and complete mastery of logistic detail; the capacity to transport large quantities of troops, weapons and supplies over difficult terrain and deploy them in the face of the enemy. Kitchener was an Engineer who made no claim to mastery on the battlefield; it was fortunate that the long campaign which culminated in the battle of Omdurman should have called above all for a display of the engineering skills.

The other quality which equipped Kitchener singularly well for the Sudanese war was his frugality. This was to be a war conducted on a shoestring and the Sirdar accepted the need for parsimony with a whole-heartedness which suggested at least a measure of relish. His cheese-paring over the quality of cloth or the cost of a roll of wire was notorious, less entertaining was his harsh resistance to any request for leave or for special facilities which might involve some official expenditure. He found it impossible to sympathize with any kind of inadequacy or ill-fortune, and his indifference to the welfare of his troops was notorious. Luckily his officers had a proper respect for his undoubted talents and made it their business to compensate for his worst deficiencies: if they had not, the army that set out on the long road to Omdurman would have been demoralised before it even started.

The first plan approved by the British government was for a limited operation, employing only the Egyptian army and penetrating no further than Dongola, two hundred miles or so up-river from Wadi Halfa. It was by no means sure, however, that Kitchener would be allowed to retain command even for so minor a foray. His comparative youth for a commander – he was forty-six; his inexperience in the field; the fact that, as Sirdar, he was responsible to the Foreign rather than the War Office; doubts as to whether, once launched on his way, he could be restrained from attempting a final settlement with the dervishes: all these were put forward as reasons for supplanting him. To his consternation the *Pall Mall Gazette* openly spoke of the decision to send a 'senior and more distinguished officer' in his stead. Cromer backed him, however, and Lord Salisbury remained loyal. When the first attack was made on the dervish outpost at Firket in June, 1896, Kitchener was still firmly in command.

Except for two British Brigades, which were to join it later, the army which Kitchener led to Firket was substantially the same as was to confront the dervishes at Omdurman more than two years later. The Egyptian and Sudanese infantry was to be reinforced in the interval but the Egyptian cavalry and that elite body, the Camel Corps, were already almost at full strength. Though some eight hundred dervishes were killed, Kitchener's victory at Firket can hardly be graced with the name of 'battle'; an outpost of the Khalifa's empire was surprised and overrun. But its political and psychological significance was greater than its military importance. For many young infantrymen in Kitchener's army it was the first proof that the dervishes were not invulnerable, that the fierce cohorts who had broken Hicks Pasha's square and stormed Khartoum could be tamed by superior discipline and fire power. For the dervishes the revelation was still more surprising, and for none more so than their commander, Osman Azrak.

Osman Azrak was one of the most fanatical and ferocious of the dervish emirs. The panache and vigour with which he had led raids deep into Egyptian territory had won him a reputation as a daring and enterprising commander; the brutality with which he treated prisoners and the Egyptian villagers had besmirched that reputation so that no enemy

Sudanese Infantry

leader was more deeply feared or hated. Slatin Pasha spoke
of him with particular loathing. His arrival in Firket had
been believed by his followers to herald the rapid destruction of the infidels, his flight from the battlefield took all
the heart out of their resistance and caused consternation
even in Omdurman. The dervishes quickly recovered from
their dismay but, for the first time, a chill tremor of doubt
had been felt. The despised 'Turks' were never again to be
dismissed as easy fodder for the dervish spears.

But it was one thing to win a skirmish only a little way
beyond the Egyptian frontier, quite another to confront
the full might of the Khalifa in the heart of his empire. The
problem was above all one of transport. Traditionally the
admirable firm of Thomas Cook, which controlled virtually all the traffic on the Egyptian Nile, was responsible
for the movements of the military. John Mason Cook,
their managing director, was known as The King Of
Upper Egypt and his renown was, indeed, close to royal.
The great Lord Cromer, being guided around one of the
provinces by Cook's dragoman, graciously consented to
be presented to a local dignitary. 'Pleased to meet any
friend of Mr Cook,' was the Egyptian's affable greeting.
This proconsul among travel agents now put all his mind
and energies into ensuring the rapid passage of the troops
and their supplies. The results were formidable. But
though Cook could convey them successfully as far as the

23

first cataract, from that point onwards the Nile imposed a series of difficult, sometimes impassable barriers to further progress. Something else was needed if transport for the army was to be guaranteed.

The battle of Omdurman, it has been said, was won in the workshops of Wadi Halfa, for it was there that the Sudan Military Railway was forged. The Nubian desert is one of the sourest and least hospitable blotches on the face of a world rich in such desolate places. 'When Allah made the Sudan,' say the Arabs, 'he laughed.' To thrust a railway across it would have been at the best of times, a hazardous enterprise. To do so at great speed, on a pitiful budget and with largely antiquated rails and rolling stock, was to tempt fortune very far. The work becomes still more exacting when it is performed in conditions of war, with the construction teams constantly exposed to the risk of attack or to seeing their painfully constructed line destroyed behind them, and the railhead towards which the line is pointing still firmly in the hands of the enemy. The feat was not merely remarkable, it was one of the great engineering enterprises of modern times. The credit for its success Kitchener shares with many people, the decision to undertake it was entirely his own. He overruled the advice of the experts, ignored the prophets of disaster. The railway was essential for the success of his operation, therefore the railway must be built. *Quod erat demonstrandum.*

A mile, two miles, even once three miles a day, the railway was forced through; sometimes more than a hundred miles from the Nile where the construction teams fondly hoped that the army was pushing on in more or less the same direction. With the temperature soaring through the nineties, supplies of water and of food precarious, dust storms making every breath a torment: the luckless engineers cursed the man who was responsible for their plight. If he had known of their curses Kitchener

Slatin Pasha and Colonel Wingate

would have been unmoved. The welfare and safety of his men was not a matter calling for serious attention. Once he found a large locomotive inexplicably not in use. He took the works manager, Sanderson, to task and was told that the boiler had cracked and might well explode if subjected to strain. 'Oh!' said the Sirdar sadly, 'That engine could pull a lot of supplies across the desert. After all, Sanderson, we aren't particular to a man or two.' The works manager thought it possible that Kitchener might be joking, but was by no means sure.

Kitchener, however, would hardly have dared expose his engineers to the threat of dervish attack if he had not been well informed about the enemy tactics and intentions. For this he was above all indebted to his director of Intelligence, Reginald Wingate. Wingate was one of those academics *manqués* who stray from time to time into military life and upset all the odds by beating the soldiers at their own game. At the age of eleven he had deserted his home in Jersey without a word to anyone or a penny in his pockets for a walking tour around the still active battle-fields of the Franco-Prussian war. This gave him a taste for army life and he startled his parents by insisting that it was to be his career. He never looked the part, being known to his fellow-officers as the White Knight because of the extraordinary miscellany of knapsacks and compasses, pots and pans, which rattled around him as he rode; but once he had entered the world of Intelligence his mastery of his métier became quickly obvious. His knowledge of Arab dialects would have graced a professor of Oriental languages; his patience was endless; his memory unique; and he delighted in the endless, subtle manoeuvrings which are the life blood of intelligence operations. With the help of Slatin Pasha, whose knowledge of and contacts in the Mahdist empire were to prove invaluable, he built up a network of spies all over the Sudan which brought him information from every village on the Nile and penetrated into the very heart of Omdurman itself. No one can predict the unpredictable and the Khalifa's fitful intuitions led him into many actions which took the British by surprise. What he *should* have done, however, was something of which Kitchener was rarely left in doubt.

In September 1896 the Anglo-Egyptian army entered Dongola. In the opinion of the government in London the campaign was over. Lord Cromer in Cairo spoke of a wait of three or four years before embarking on another step. Only Kitchener was determined to push on at once. He knew that if the impetus he had built up were dissipated, morale would slump; the efficiency of the army deteriorate and final victory vanish into the distance, perhaps for

26

ever. He hastened to London to bring pressure on the recalcitrant ministers, armed with a sensational report furnished by the obliging Wingate. The Sudanese and Abyssinians were plotting a joint descent on the invaders. Egypt itself was threatened. Worst of all, the French had got their fingers into the pie and were planning to extend their zone of influence across the upper Nile. With some reluctance ministers accepted that sooner or later a further advance would have to be undertaken and that the sooner would probably prove the cheaper. 'I am no believer,' admitted the Chancellor of the Exchequer, 'in the mission of even so powerful a country as this to redress the wrongs of humanity all over the world. But here is a case in which the task is ready to our hand.' Still, however, the task was to be limited. At the strong urging of Cromer the target for 1897 was fixed as Berber, still nearly two hundred miles by river from Khartoum.

Kitchener would have hesitated to venture even so far unless he had had complete command of the river. The fact that he enjoyed this advantage was due, above all, to his fleet of gunboats. These lumbering, armour-plated Leviathans, slow in movement, inelegant in lines, still carried an armoury capable of demolishing any Arab fort which they might encounter along the banks of the Nile. Kitchener started with four of them, antiquated by the standards of what was to come, but still quite formidable enough to have maintained Gordon indefinitely in Khartoum if he had had the good luck to include them in his armoury. Then came a new and yet more fearsome model, designed specifically for the campaign, crated in a myriad of containers and carried laboriously by train, camel and steamer up the Nile to the assembly point. One hundred and forty feet long and 24 feet wide, these boats could steam at twelve miles an hour and draw only 39 inches of water. Each carried a twelve-pounder quick-firing gun, two six-pounders, a howitzer, four Maxim guns and, what was to prove as useful as anything, a battery of searchlights. They provided the most formidable concentration of fire power in the Sudan.

The new gunboats were Kitchener's delight. When the construction of the first boat, the *Zafir*, began in the improvised dock-yard at Kosheh, he visited the work almost every day and plagued the engineers to make quicker progress. His particular hobby was to drive in rivets, and a special A.D.C. was detailed to follow him, surreptitiously marking with a piece of chalk those rivets honoured by the Sirdar's hand. A technician then moved round in his wake, discreetly making good the defects in his commander's handiwork. Disaster was to overtake the *Zafir* on her first excursion. The stern paddle had hardly begun to revolve before there was a loud explosion, clouds of steam, and the engine stopped. A cylinder had burst and it was to take several weeks and much frustration before the new giant joined its colleagues at Dongola.

In the advance to Berber the gunboats were everywhere. They were commanded by young naval officers who had been posted to the Sudan above all for their capacity to act in isolation and on their own initiative. Among them was the twenty-nine year old Lt David Beatty, later to win still greater renown as Admiral of the Fleet and a hero of Jutland. He had already narrowly escaped drowning when his ship, the *El Teb*, had been dashed against a rock and sunk while trying to pass the Fourth Cataract. Now the whole flotilla was ranging along the open water between the cataract and Berber: attacking enemy formations, ferrying supplies to General Hunter's flying column, picking up the wounded or, more frequently, the victims of fever and heat-stroke. Their presence meant that no dervish troops along the banks of the Nile could feel themselves secure; at any moment the dreaded iron monsters might swoop down and blast them prematurely to paradise.

In August, 1897, General Hunter's advance-guard of 2700 men and 1300 camels took the dervish forces at Abu Hamed by surprise and stormed the town with the loss of two officers and twenty-five men. It seemed inevitable that the enemy would make a more determined stand at Berber and all plans were made on the basis that this would prove to be a major battle-field. Then a group of loyalist tribesmen penetrated as far as the town and reported the astonishing news that the garrison had fled. Hurriedly Kitchener sent four gunboats with a battalion of Sudanese to complete the occupation. Now he found himself faced with the moment of decision which he had believed to be still several months ahead. To strike beyond Berber would be pointless unless it was intended to thrust right home to the Khalifa's capital at Omdurman; yet Kitchener was resolved not to attempt this without the reinforcement of British troops. Anyway, it was still far from sure that Cromer in Cairo or the government in Whitehall would sanction any such adventure. Perhaps the most troublesome consideration, in Kitchener's eyes, was the risk that, if British reinforcements did arrive, they would bring with them a general of such seniority that the command of the expedition would fall to him. In July, 1897, General Grenfell, the previous Sirdar, arrived back in Cairo to take over the British army of occupation; 'the army of no-occupation' as Kitchener sourly called it. Was this the first step in a War Office plot to wrest from the present Sirdar the glory of final victory?

For several months everything was uncertain. It was Wingate who broke the deadlock. With a sense of timing that the suspicious might feel a little too felicitous he now revealed that he had received sensational news. The Khalifa with all his forces was about to emerge from Omdurman and sally north. More than a hundred thousand men would march to all-out attack. The Anglo-Egyptian army could hardly hope to resist such a host.

Ignominious flight seemed the only alternative to destruction. At this moment of indecision Cromer stuck loyally by his commander. He argued with London that a brigade of British troops should immediately be sent up the Nile from the forces now in Egypt, that further reinforcements should be sent from England and that Kitchener should continue to lead the expedition. Salisbury agreed. The penultimate phase in the River War was about to open.

The omniscient spy-master was either deceived or wilfully self-deceiving. The Khalifa had watched aghast as the Anglo-Egyptian force ground steadily towards him. Who were these infidels? He knew that there were two powerful emirs in Britain, one of whom seemed to be for war, the other for peace. Had the aggressor triumphed, was the more pacific of the emirs even now lying in chains in some London dungeon? Were these the same men as had run away fifteen years before when they found that they were too late to relieve Khartoum? If so, would they not once more be daunted by a show of force? Common sense and his bolder commanders insisted that he should advance in force to destroy the 'Turks' – as all Europeans were generally described – before their own army had been built up to its full strength. But the Khalifa Abdullahi had dreamed a dream in which he saw himself riding into battle on the plains of Kerreri before Omdurman, had heard the cries of victory and the wail of the defeated, had seen the plains white with the skulls of the slaughtered infidels. The Khalifa would not sally out himself but nor would he suffer the Turks to advance unopposed to their destruction. He settled for a compromise. He sent forward the Emir Mahmud with some 16,000 men to recapture Berber. If the invaders were men of straw then Mahmud would be more than a match for them; if they were indeed the fighting force he feared, then only 16,000 men would have been lost and, incidentally, a truculent and somewhat insubordinate member of his inner circle conveniently

General Gatacre

disposed of. As a prescription for disaster the strategy could hardly have been improved.

By the end of January, 1898, the first battalions of the Warwickshire Regiment, the Lincolnshire Regiment and the Cameron Highlanders had arrived in the Sudan. In February, when it became evident that Mahmud was advancing to attack, the first battalion of the Seaforth Highlanders joined them at the front. The first British Brigade was under the command of General Gatacre. Kitchener was respected by all, worshipped by a few, and too far above the mob to be genuinely loved or hated. Gatacre, too, was respected but it is doubtful if anyone worshipped him and the number of his enemies was legion. He was an electric-saw of a man – rasping, fretting, perpetually active – whose ambition was to do every job in the Brigade himself. From an indecently early dawn until late at night his spare, wiry form was everywhere, nagging, interfering, supervising every facet of the daily life of an army on the move. The men called him 'General Back-acher', but recognised that his activities were generally benevolent and on the whole thought well of him. The officers called him 'Fatacre', bitterly resented his inability to let them get on with their job in their own way and considered him a tactless and aggravating bounder. Kitchener appreciated him. He liked a subordinate who would not interfere in the higher strategy or expect a large share of the glory, he respected industry and efficiency and he did not care twopence for the injured sensibilities of his officers. Indeed, on the whole, he probably thought that their sensibilities were the better for being outraged: a complacent officer was well on the way to being an idle and an inefficient one.

The British Brigade was soon to be engaged in battle. Mahmud had by now been joined by Osman Digna, ruler of the Hadendoa – the notorious 'fuzzy-wuzzies' – and one of the oldest and certainly the wiliest of the Khalifa's emirs. In 1884 Osman had been prominent in the rout of General Valentine Baker at El Teb but since then his reputation had been more for survival than for victory. By his less kindly compatriots he was, indeed, known as 'The Grand Master of the Art of Flight'. Flight was an art for which Mahmud had little use and that belligerent commander viewed the arrival of his new ally with little enthusiasm. Left to himself he would probably have flung himself against the strengthened Anglo-Egyptian force without more ado; left to *himself*, Osman

Burials after the battle of the Atbara

Digna would certainly have avoided action altogether; as it was their force, depleted by desertions and deaths on the march to some 12,000 infantry and 3000 cavalry, wedged itself against the bank of the river Atbara, a tributary of the Nile, and waited to see what Kitchener would do.

Kitchener dithered. Faced with the need to take a crucial and conceivably disastrous decision, he referred the issue to Lord Cromer in Cairo. Should he or should he not attack, he asked the surprised proconsul. Before Cromer or the War Office could advise, however, the Sirdar repented of his vacillation. Since Mahmud was not proving gentleman enough to dash himself to destruction against the British guns, then the guns must go to Mahmud. At dawn on April 8, Good Friday, the artillery opened fire on the thorn hedge or 'zariba' which guarded the dervish position. At 7.15 a.m. the troops took up assault positions. Half an hour later the bombardment ceased and at 8 a.m. with bands playing, pipes skirling and shouts of

'Remember Gordon', Kitchener's infantry swept down upon the enemy. The Camerons led the attack. At the head of the British Brigade they slow marched towards the zariba, stopping from time to time to let off devastating volleys, then marching on again with the calmness and regularity of a parade-ground exercise. Within half an hour it was all over, the dervish zariba had been overrun, Mahmud was a prisoner, Osman Digna had fled once more. Three thousand dervishes were dead and many hundreds captured against a total casualty list for the Sirdar's army of less than 600. But many brave men whom the army could ill spare had perished, and the Highland regiments in particular had suffered sadly with three officers and eighteen men killed and six officers and sixty-six men wounded.

Kitchener's tactics had not been distinguished by subtlety: to advance in line abreast on a fortified enemy position would have been a tactic within the grasp of every schoolboy. In the circumstances, nevertheless, it was probably the right thing to do – against an enemy armed only with Remington elephant-guns and old brass muzzle-loaders a measure of crudity could be permitted. Militarily the action had been wholly effective. The dervish army had been virtually destroyed. Nothing of consequence now lay between Kitchener and his final target. On April 14, mounted in triumph on a white horse, he made a formal entry into Berber with the wretched Mahmud, hands tied behind him, dragged at the tails of the cavalry. Gordon had not yet been avenged but a first payment had been made on the long outstanding debt. Now it was on to Omdurman.

Kitchener by von Herkomer

CHAPTER II

The Grand Advance

IT had taken twenty-three months for Kitchener's army to advance from the Sudanese border; it was to take as many days from the arrival of the last reinforcements to the closing of the campaign at Omdurman. There was, however, to be an interval of several months before the final phase was reached. The season of the year made this delay desirable; it was not till the end of July that the Nile would be navigable as far as Khartoum and Kitchener had no intention of doing without his simplest and surest means of transport, let alone the support of his precious gun-boats. Even if the river had been in full spate, however, he would still have wished to pause at the Atbara so as to push the railhead further forward, build up supplies and allow the last reinforcements to arrive from England. Victory was too rich a prize to run any risk of losing it for the want of a ha'pennyworth of tar.

As soon as the last of Mahmud's fugitives had been rounded up, the expeditionary force went into summer quarters at various points along the Nile between Atbara and Berber. Most of the senior officers went on leave. Many of the junior officers did the same; to Cairo, at least, and often to Europe and to England. The other ranks were left to languish in the full blast of a Sudanese summer, drilling hectically in the early morning to remind themselves that they were soldiers and contemplating the waters of the Nile for the rest of the day. For the officers there was a little desultory shooting and fishing of a kind. One monster of eighty-four pounds was landed. The species was indeterminate and the taste was foul – Nilotic mud with a faint tang of mustard – but the achievement still gave rise to justifiable pride. For the men there was always the brothel, though this had its hazards. The Lancashire Fusiliers, who were among the first of the reinforcements to arrive, had eleven cases of venereal disease reported within a week. Since one of the more active prostitutes claimed to have satisfied sixty-two clients in twenty-four hours, the casualty rate does not seem extravagant. The remarkable thing is that the morale of the army remained high and neither the physique nor the discipline of the soldiers seriously deteriorated.

Kitchener himself took only a month away and went no further than Cairo. He was in conspicuously good humour. He 'is inclined to think that his force will be inconveniently large,' Cromer recorded, but no one noticed that his demands for reinforcements or supplies were any the less exigent as a result. His leave over, he hastened back to Abadia, a village twenty miles north of Berber which the railway had now reached. Here it was proposed to assemble his newest and most cherished acquisition – three super gun-boats, of totally novel design, carrying each a massive armament of two $12\frac{1}{2}$-pounder Maxim-Nordenfeldts, one 12-pounder Krupp, a 4-inch howitzer and four Maxims. The work was entrusted to Major W.S. – or more commonly 'Monkey' – Gordon, a nephew of the murdered general. This highly competent officer was given no peace by his commander, who haunted the dockyard, offering unwanted advice and unmerited criticism. He could not resist a chance to interfere, however inadequate his grounds for doing so. Once Gordon was literally buried beneath a tangled pile of sleepers which depended for its equilibrium on one strategically placed girder. To this girder a stout rope was still attached. To his dismay he suddenly heard Kitchener's bellow: 'Hurry up, men! What are you waiting for? Pull on that rope!' Faced with obliteration he threw aside decorum and screamed abuse at the general.

The gunboat 'Melik'

Kitchener turned to Wingate who was with him. 'Perhaps we should go and have breakfast,' he commented resignedly.

But in spite of everything the new gun-boats, 'Monkey Gordon's Greyhounds' as they were unkindly nicknamed, were not a success. Their guns were formidable and their armour more than adequate, but they were so under-powered that they could only advance at two knots against the current and their draught was too shallow to allow them any useful role in towing barges. They were to come into their own during the battle itself but were more trouble than they were worth in the preparatory stages. Gordon, for his pains, was given the doubtful prize of command of one of them, the *Melik*. He was one of the seventeen Engineer officers whom Kitchener managed to deploy around him in the closing stages of the campaign.

When the Sirdar was not plaguing Gordon at Abadia he was at Fort Atbara, supervising the build up of supplies. Never was his determination to do all his own staff work more clearly illustrated. His favourite haunt was the *nuzl*, the area near the river where all the new equipment was accumulated. 'He is gone nuzzling again,' was the resigned reply of his A.D.C. Jimmy Watson whenever his master was sought for. And he nuzzled to good effect. Never can commander have known more precisely the material at his disposition and the means of carrying it from place to place and in few campaigns can such mastery of detail have been put to better purpose.

And so the summer wore on and the officers began to return to their regiments. Felix Ready, a captain with the 2nd Egyptian Battalion, was on his way back from a relaxing month in the flesh-pots of Southern England. He claimed to have set a record in that he left London on July 6 and was in command of an advance outpost at Nasri Island, only sixty-five miles from Omdurman, three weeks later on July 27. He travelled up from Wadi Halfa with Slatin Pasha and found him 'great fun and very anxious to catch the Khalifa'. Many people doubted whether the dervishes would stand and fight; Slatin was confident that there would be a great battle on the plains in front of Omdurman. Ready and many others offered a nightly prayer that Slatin might be proved correct.

Now the last wave of reinforcements steamed up the river: the 2nd British Brigade. The 1st Battalion of the Grenadier Guards arrived from Gibraltar; the 1st Battalion of the Northumberland Fusiliers – the Fighting Fifth – and the 2nd Battalion of the Lancashire Fusiliers, from Cairo; and the 2nd Battalion of the Rifle Brigade from Malta. As cavalry support came the 21st Lancers from Cairo and Kitchener's artillery was supplemented by a new battery of Howitzers which fired giant shells charged with lyddite, two large 40-pounder guns and a second Maxim battery. With substantial reinforcements also arriving for the Egyptian Division, the Sirdar could feel confident that, whether or not his army was 'inconveniently large', he had enough power to settle with the Khalifa. With the arrival of the 2nd Brigade, Gatacre handed over command of the 1st Brigade to Brigadier General Wauchope and took over the British Division. So far as the unfortunate Brigadiers were concerned the change was more apparent than real. Wauchope and Lyttelton, his counterpart with the 1st Brigade, found that Gatacre acted in effect as his own brigadier and took upon himself to decide even the slightest details of daily administration.

The 1st Brigade at the Atbara had suffered from two striking deficiencies of equipment. The first, literally crippling, was that their boots were soled with an unpleasing substance which rasped the skin like sandpaper and, under pressure, crumbled like cardboard; the fruit of the Sirdar's determination to shop only in the cheapest market. The second was that the nickel-plated Lee-Metford bullet, though accurate in flight, seemed to cause only irritation to the more distant of the dervishes at whom it was aimed. By the time the build up was complete the boots had largely been replaced and what were left of the Lee-Metford bullets had been filed down into a less accurate but more lethal Dum-Dum. The 2nd Brigade, in no way the victim of the Sirdar's lust for economy, were anyway better equipped for the campaign, even if their uniforms would have seemed unbearably heavy to later exponents of the art of desert warfare.

All ranks wore regulation khaki, the only splash of colour being found in the coloured cotton patches and regimental badges worn on the khaki helmet covers. The Rifle Brigade wore a dark green patch, bleached by the sun to a shade of dried-pea yellow; the Lancashire Fusiliers a square yellow patch; the Fighting Fifth a diagonal red band round the helmet; the Grenadiers a gay red and blue rosette; the Lincolns a plain square white patch; the Warwicks a red square; the Seaforths a white plume, the 'duck's tuft'; and the Camerons a 'true blue' square patch. Inevitably the new arrivals came in for some criticism from the older hands, and their efforts to guard against the desert sun were the subject of much derision. It was noticed that the Rifle Brigade had equipped all its men with a blue veil and goggles. 'It really is funny,' commented Felix Ready, 'what an unnecessary guy they make of poor Tommy!'

In spite of all this and of the appalling heat and discomfort of the journey up, morale among the Rifles was particularly high. The officers' mess had a banquet on board their cattle truck the night before it arrived at the Atbara. The menu says more for their ingenuity than either their cooking or their French:

Hors d'oeuvres	*Variés*
Pôtage	*Consommé a la Nubie*
Poisson	*Sardines au Nil. Sauce poussière*
Entré	*Boeuf au tyrant lâche* [freely translated as 'bully beef']
Desserts	*Fruits assortis au fer-blanc*
Vins	*Eau de Nil 1898 (Brut)*
	Whisky écossais 1888 (Fin)
	Jus de citron à la Rose

After the banquet the train halted briefly while all ranks joined in a sing-song. A 'very clever set of verses on the campaign up to date' was composed and recited by Rifleman Gibbons. After that came *Home Sweet Home, The Boys of the Old Brigade, Soldiers of the Queen* and *Old Folks at Home*. The hit of the evening, however, was a ballad which had already established itself as a favourite with the whole expeditionary force. Called *Roll on to Khartoum*, its rousing chorus ran:

> '*Then roll on, boys, roll on to Khartoum,*
> *March ye and fight ye by night or by day,*
> *Hasten the hour of the Dervishes' doom,*
> *Gordon avenge in old England's way!*'

Not surprisingly the arrival of these ebullient new-comers – swaggering about the encampment and boasting that, now they had arrived, the hash of the Khalifa would quickly be settled – was greeted rather sourly by the older hands who had marched and fought from the frontier to the Atbara. The Guards were said to be pampered choco-late soldiers who would quickly melt in the Sudanese sun. The Rifles, notoriously made up of 'cockneys without constitutions', would be even less able to cope with the rigours ahead. Even the 1st Brigade, who themselves had only arrived a few months before, spoke scornfully of their new comrades in arms as 'week-end trippers'. Cap-tain Egerton, a young officer with the Seaforths who left a lively account of the campaign, railed at the sort of officer who arrived on a Wednesday, expected to fight a battle on a Friday and to leave again on Saturday, 'receiv-ing for arduous services a mention in despatches'. The veterans of the Egyptian army were still more derisive. Felix Ready was outraged when a young puppy from the Guards complained about the horrors of the journey from Cairo, nearly fourteen days in the train. 'He never thought that it had taken the majority of fellows out here two years, working all the time, to get here.' Worse still, they were amateurs. Prince Christian Victor was posted as staff-officer for the gun-boats: 'I suppose he knows as much about a gun-boat as my foot, he has never been on the Nile and doesn't know a word of Arabic.'

The 2nd Brigade by no means acknowledged their inferiority, on the contrary they heartily reciprocated the contempt. Colonel Hatton, the unpopular but capable colonel of the Grenadiers, felt that the so-called 'seasoned' battalions were in fact played out. Incessant marching in the hot sun had sapped their strength instead of building it up and the new-comers had far greater reserves of fitness. The next weeks seemed to prove him right. During the harsh marches across the desert in the period preceding Omdurman less men fell out from the Grenadiers and the Rifle Brigade than from any other British battalion and more than twice as many from the 1st Brigade as from the 2nd.

Another regiment whose arrival gave rise to a certain amount of mockery was the 21st Lancers. As Hussars the 21st had been in existence for more than thirty years, yet they bore no battle honour, and had not, indeed, been involved in even the most trivial skirmish. 'Thou shalt not kill,' was said to be their regimental motto. The joke was not appreciated by their gallant yet strikingly stupid commanding officer, Colonel Martin. He was resolved that this time the Lancers should see action, whatever the circumstances, and had imbued his officers with the same reckless determination. 'These men are regular Thrusters,' remarked an officer of a line-regiment with what appeared to be a mixture of admiration and apprehension.

No one who was used to seeing the Lancers on the parade ground at Cairo would have recognised them now. Dressed in 'Christmas-tree order', with an incredible miscellany of packs and packages slung around their bodies and broad canvas shades hanging from their helmets, they looked more like some Egyptian child's nightmare of men from outer space than dashing cavalry-men on their way to battle. They had had a rough journey from Cairo, the horses still more so, and they looked a sadly shop-soiled lot when their barges pulled up to the bank of the Atbara. Major Bagot, a Grenadier officer with a keen eye and frequently caustic pen, was dismayed at what he saw. One horse, apparently with sun-stroke, 'jumped up in the air and overboard – as if he had been shot, and disappeared'. Several of the men looked wistfully after the disappearing animal, as if they felt that it was well out of its sufferings and that they were more than half inclined to follow the same line of escape.

One young officer from the 4th Hussars, who had been attached to the 21st at the urgent request of Lord Wolseley, formed a very low opinion of his new comrades. 'The 21st Lancers are not on the whole a good business,' wrote the twenty-four year old Winston Churchill to his mother, 'and I would much rather have been attached to Egyptian cavalry staff – they hate all the number of attached officers and some of them take little pains to conceal their dislike. As you may imagine this annoys rather than disturbs me.' The arrogance of the last phrase explains in part why the Lancer officers looked askance at this egregious cuckoo in their nest, especially when they realised that he was under contract to *The Morning Post* and therefore had a foot in a camp which, if not actually enemy, was at least deeply suspect.

But Churchill had contrived to irritate not merely the Lancer officers but almost everyone he met. On the boat across the Mediterranean, when he should by all the rules have listened deferentially to his seniors, 'in the intervals of graphic accounts of his recent experiences on the Indian frontier, he supplied us with luminous information as to the principle and practice of Tory democracy'. In the train on the way up from Cairo his fellow-officers were speculating how many among them were likely to be mentioned in despatches. Churchill told them there was only one part of the despatch in which they could hope to find mention. 'They asked what part. I replied, "The casualty list!"' It is perhaps hardly surprising that he was made to

Lieutenant Molyneux and Lieutenant Churchill in the Sudan

travel a large part of the distance underneath the seat. 'Saw that little prig Winston Churchill today,' stormed Bagot a few days later. 'He makes me sick.' He made most of the British officers sick; not least the Sirdar who had objected to his coming and now refused to receive him, even though he came armed with a personal letter of recommendation from the Prime Minister.

Sixteen 'so-called representatives of the press' have arrived, reported the veteran correspondent of the *Daily Telegraph* Bennet Burleigh. '. . . some of them represented anything

45

but journals or journalism, the name of the newspaper being used merely as a cover for notoriety and medal hunting.' Churchill was undoubtedly one of the 'so-called representatives' whom Burleigh – quite unfairly as it turned out – had in mind, but there were other amateurs among the band. Ernest Bennett, for instance, special correspondent of the *Westminster Gazette*, was a don from Hertford College who only marked the last of the Trinity Term's examination papers as the boat-train steamed into Folkestone station. Querulous and pedantic, he felt the officers' mess a poor substitute for the senior common room and took no pains to conceal his confidence in his own superiority. Henry Cross was a schoolmaster who had somehow been accredited to the *Manchester Guardian*. He had rowed five in the Varsity boat ten years before, but his physique served for little in the Sudan; he hobbled from the hospital barge to the battle-field, but was dead of enteric fever a fortnight later. Frankie Rhodes, correspondent of *The Times* and elder brother of the great Cecil, had been a soldier till two years before, when he was cashiered for his involvement in the Jameson Raid.

As well as Burleigh, however, there were other seasoned professionals among the group. Frank Scudamore, of the *Daily News*, was a diminutive freak who, in spite of the strict restrictions on officers' baggage, managed to bring with him to the battle-field not only beer and sparkling wines but an ice machine as well. He was so small that, when all officers were ordered to dismount under dervish fire, he alone remained on his horse on the plea that, otherwise, he could not see to do his job. But the doyen of the press corps was probably Fred Villiers of the *Globe* and *Illustrated London News*. For nearly forty years, wherever there was serious trouble on the globe's surface, Villiers was rarely far away. Shot at, ship-wrecked, assailed with spears and swords, tumbling down mountains, shooting rapids, he miraculously survived more or less

46

unscathed. For reasons obscure but not wholly unconnected with his marked aptitude for self-advertisement, Villiers made the journey from Hagir to Omdurman with a green, battered, but triumphantly unpunctured bicycle. The gesture was a fine one but his more cynical colleagues noted that, as often as not, Villiers was mounted on a donkey while an unlucky servant was left to wheel the bicycle.

Professional or amateur, veteran or tyro, Kitchener hated the lot of them. He had tried to have all the correspondents confined to the base area but had been made to cancel the order after the proprietor of *The Times* had appealed to the prime minister. Now he made his opinion of them manifest by treating them with animosity and doing them every mischief in his power. Wingate, reluctantly detailed as censor, did his best to appease them but he had an up-hill task. Two or three days before the battle a group of journalists were clustered outside the Sirdar's tent in expectation of a promised statement. Kitchener kept them waiting for an hour in the sun, then thrust his way angrily through them with: 'Get out of my way, you drunken swabs!' His loathing was reciprocated. In their published despatches the correspondents treated the Sirdar with awed admiration but their private letters and diaries tell a very different story.

'Now that Eddie Wortley and Winston Churchill are here,' wrote Major Bagot sourly on August 16, 'all will be well.' Major the Hon. Edward Montagu-Stuart-Wortley, to give him his full designation, was to command the most freakish and least reliable element of Kitchener's army. An eccentric, an Arabist of distinction and a veteran of the abortive expedition to rescue Gordon, he was an obvious choice to be put in charge of the 'Friendlies', a highly irregular force of about 2500 Jaalin, Bisherin, Hadendoa and other reputedly well-disposed Arabs. The principal weaknesses of this body were that their armament was, to say the least, motley – consisting of old flint-and-steel muskets, elephant guns, ancient muzzle-loading pistols and the inevitable spears, swords and daggers; their discipline was no more than sketchy; and their friendliness was unlikely to survive the first indication that they might have chosen the losing side.

The idea was that Wortley would lead his irregulars up the east bank of the Nile, more or less keeping pace with the spearhead of Kitchener's army on the west bank, and clear out of the way any dervish opposition. Eventually they would establish themselves on the river opposite Omdurman and prepare a site on which the Artillery could ensconce itself and bombard the Khalifa's capital at leisure. It was believed that there were only a thousand or so Mahdists on the eastern bank of the Nile; what happened if in fact a substantial dervish army had crossed the river was something which Wortley preferred not to contemplate.

One thing on which everyone, from Sirdar to subaltern, from cavalry swell to Rifle Brigade ranker, was agreed on was that the Atbara camp was a hell on earth after which even death at the hands of the dervishes would seem a merciful relief. George Jeffreys, a second-lieutenant in the Grenadier Guards, who was one day to become Colonel of the Regiment, had his first taste of the horrors to come the very night of his arrival on August 8. Hardly had the exhausted troops slumped into sleep when the wind began to rise. In no time a storm was raging. 'Half the tents in camp soon down and property of all sorts flying about. We hopped out and held on to our tent pole for dear life, and fortunately kept it up. Woke in the morning with eyes, mouth and nose choked with sand, miserable and unrefreshed . . .' Jeffreys was a notably cheerful, indeed frivolous young man, but even for him this was a little much.

48

Sand and dust was indeed the constant backcloth against which the plagues of Egypt performed their phrenetic dance. Flies of unequalled malice and persistence who relished the fumes even of the strongest tobacco; scorpions who seemed to nestle in every blanket and lurk attentively in every boot; a huge hairy yellow creature called by the locals *Abu Shelek*, 'The Father of Spiders'; asps eight inches long whose bite was potent enough to kill a camel; the thorn of the *nebek*, curling inward, strong and sharp enough to rip open a man's leg and embed itself like a fish-hook deep below the skin: these were among the delights of the Atbara. Nile boils, ulcerated throats, sunstroke, apoplexy, above all enteric fever; these were the penalties which struck down the unwary or the unfortunate.

The troops, of course, made the best of it. They even made a virtue of their afflictions. Matching scorpions against spiders was a favourite diversion. The Warwickshire Pet, a huge spider and the pride of the regiment, was undisputed champion of the First Brigade. The Camerons, however, had a scorpion, The Slogger, which they believed might dethrone him. At last the pair were matched. The spider seemed over-confident, sluggish in its reactions; the scorpion was on top of its form. A sudden dash, a flurry, and the battle was over almost before it had begun. The Cameron Slogger was the new champion. But such pastimes could not distract the troops for long from their dismal situation. Every day spent at the Atbara encampment was a day too many.

Then, on the morning of August 13, 1898, it was suddenly realised that the Sirdar's tents were empty. Without a word to anyone except his most immediate staff he had dictated a final despatch, boarded a gun-boat and was gone. With his disappearance a mood of new expectancy swept the army. The build-up was over, the last advance was under way.

CHAPTER III

The Final March

IN fact, as would have been noted by any member of the British Division who paid attention to the movements of the Egyptian and Sudanese troops, Kitchener's departure was only one more, if dramatic, step in a movement which had begun several weeks before. All the evidence suggested that the Khalifa would make his final stand at or near Omdurman. The object was, therefore, to find a convenient site to which the bulk of the infantry could advance by boat, which would be far enough from Omdurman to rule out the possibility of a sudden swoop by the dervishes when only a few battalions were assembled, yet which was not so far that the army could not march the remaining distance comfortably in a few days. The choice fell on Wad Hamed, an unmemorable hamlet some fifty-eight miles north of Omdurman. There was still much to be done, however, before the move of the main force could get properly under way.

Even before the Grenadier Guards had arrived at the Atbara, Captain Felix Ready, with a company from the 2nd Egyptian Battalion, was installed at Nasri Island, a mere ten miles from Wad Hamed. Here an advance supply depot was assembled and great piles of timber accumulated to feed into the maws of the voracious gun-boats and steamers. In the intervals of supervising such labours and shooting at the evening flights of grouse – 'Scotland could not beat it,' he noted with approval after he and another officer had killed twenty brace in an hour and a half on the Twelfth of August – Ready interrogated deserters from the Khalifa's forces. 'They say the blacks are all very hungry and the Khalifa is nearly off his head,' he recorded. 'He goes down to the river and beats the water with his sword and still preaches that the dogs (us) will perish like flies before the sacred tomb of the Mahdi.'

Along the banks of the Nile units of the Egyptian cavalry and the camel corps were similarly amassing great heaps of timber in anticipation of the coming of the fleet. If he had thought about the matter at all, the average British soldier would certainly have considered such menial labour entirely appropriate to his allies. Prospero Kitchener must command his Calibans and, after all, one could hardly expect a white man to toil in this way in the African sun. The Egyptian and Sudanese soldiery were generally regarded by the British troops with contempt; usually tolerant, sometimes even affectionate, but contempt none the less. The attitude, indeed, embraced far more than just the military. 'Your Arab is picturesque but poisonous;' wrote the stalwart Bennet Burleigh. 'A fine specimen of a man, though his usefulness in the economy of things is not apparent . . .' The native troops, Arabs and negroes alike, were 'Sambos', plucky enough when well commanded and no doubt decent in their pagan way, but totally lacking the character and calm resolution of European troops. They were, if not sub-human, decidedly sub-British: 'These animals do not suffer like us,' as another war correspondent consolingly reflected when confronted by a dervish, both legs shattered and stomach perforated, crawling the two miles or so to the Nile in search of water.

The attitude differed little when the Egyptian or Sudanese in question was an officer and thus, in a manner of speaking, a gentleman. Though most of the locally recruited battalions had at least some British officers, there were also Albanians, Circassians and Turks as well as Egyptian and Sudanese. But though the *bimbashi*, or major, and even the *kaimakan*, or colonel, might be non-British, there was always at least one British sergeant as instructor, 'technically subordinate to the native officers but in fact leaving them in no doubt about their superiority. He marches always with the men: "Where a nigger can go, I can go!"' Even the war correspondents felt themselves a class apart. The insufferable Ernest Bennett was vastly offended when he found that he was supposed to travel from the Atbara camp to Wad Hamed on a native *gyassa* towed by a gun-boat. Regrettably Colonel Wingate 'took pity on our abject position and we were permitted to leave the society of the Gyppy officers and have our meals on the upper deck'. Luckily the British officers actually in charge of native battalions treated their men with greater respect, otherwise there might well have been many defections to the Khalifa when battle was joined. As it was there were twenty or so desertions to the enemy while the army was at Wad Hamed, the deserters being tempted by – Bennett again – 'a life of eating, sleeping and fighting; an ideal existence in the eyes of an animal like the average Sudanese soldier'.

The approved scale for the loading of the barges was that a given space should be occupied by one horse, four British soldiers or seven natives. It should not be imagined from this, however, that the British troops travelled in anything approaching comfort. The Sirdar was determined that the move should be completed by August 25 at the latest. If this involved overloading the boats then the boats must be overloaded. The four steamers, each towing two double-decked troop barges and two Arab *gyassas*, or sailing boats, were the main means of transport, but the gun-boats, except for the under-powered new arrivals, were also pressed into service. 'The last fortnight has been a regular nightmare,' wrote Beatty crossly, 'dashing up and down the river carrying troops, Egyptian, Sudanese and British, and for the most troublesome beggars, give me the latter. They are a terror, want everything done for them, grumble . . . I first trotted up the Warwicks and then the Lancashire Fusiliers, the latter a most meritorious crew – didn't give a damn for anyone.'

Everyone had to be crammed into the boats, in defiance of all the normal regulations. An agonised engineer officer pointed out to the Sirdar that the Plimsoll line on one of the steamers was already well under water. 'Plimsoll's dead,' observed Kitchener laconically. Another officer was instructed to cram 350 men on to a barge designed for half that number. By a combination of brutality and skill he got 280 aboard, then reported back that it was physically impossible for him to take any more. 'Oh, I think you can,' said the Sirdar with a mildness which deceived nobody. 'Come back and let me know when you have done it.' The men were got on board and the boat still floated. 'When they get to the other end,' remarked an awe-struck observer, 'it will be like unpacking a new box of biscuits. They'll have to pull the middle man out with a jerk before any of the others can move.'

The Seaforths were one of the first British regiments to arrive at Wad Hamed. Their journey had been uncomfortable but uneventful: except, reported Captain Egerton, for 'a huge lizard, as big as a young crocodile', which got aboard one of the barges and created something near panic on the crowded decks. The 2nd Brigade quickly followed in the wake of the 1st, the Grenadiers arriving on August 18. Young George Jeffreys had amused himself during the journey by observing the 'enormous flocks of water birds, geese, pelicans, storks, ducks etc. besides beautiful little parrokeets and scarlet birds like humming birds'. His seniors, he noticed, mostly curled themselves uncomfortably around the crowded decks and tried to sleep the journey through.

No one fared quite as ill as the last contingent of the Rifle Brigade which got left so far behind that it had to overshoot Wad Hamed and rejoin the army the other side of the Sixth Cataract at Jebel Royan. As the steamer swung into the Shabluka gorge, Captain Rawlinson, a singularly intrepid officer and a great favourite of Kitchener's, who was later to win glory as a General and a Lord, was vividly and unpleasantly reminded of the Khyber Pass. '. . . If you can imagine the Pass filled with a roaring torrent it will give you some idea of the appearance of the cataract. It is the rush and swirl of the huge volume of water which is the impressive feature of the Shabluka. The dark chocolate-coloured water dashes down in eddies and whirlpools with a force which makes it impossible for any but the most lightly laden steamers to keep in mid-stream, and everywhere except in mid-stream there are rocks which will tear the bottom out of any craft which strikes them . . . I was in a blue funk. We just shaved the murderous looking rocks of one promontory, with barely a foot to spare, to dash across the torrent into the slack water on the other bank, only to shave another rock which almost swamped our side. At each shore I could not help thinking what a crash would mean, for there would have been little chance of any of our 400 men coming out alive from that seething torrent.'

In fact all the steamers and gun-boats eventually passed the Sixth Cataract without disaster, so the peril was perhaps not quite so imminent as Rawlinson imagined. To a poor infantryman, however, unused to the terrors of the deep, it must have seemed painfully alarming. Certainly there can have been few Riflemen who would not willingly have traded their place on the boats with one of the cavalrymen wending their way placidly along the bank.

There can have been even fewer cavalrymen who would not have jumped at the chance to make the exchange. The camel corps, the Egyptian cavalry and the 21st Lancers had been left to manage as best they could on the gruelling march across the desert. The 21st Lancers had left the Atbara camp at dawn on August 16. The horses, out of condition after nearly two weeks of congested life on the barges, found it unfairly arduous to march a full day with seventeen stone of Lancer and equipment on their backs. The soft feet of the baggage camels were cut to shreds by the stones and thorns. The men themselves, short of water, inadequately protected from the sun, wilted in the intense heat of a Sudanese summer. As the barges swept up the Nile the cramped and weary soldiers aboard would see forlorn little groups of Lancers beckoning to them from the bank: two or three men tending to a comrade who had collapsed with sunstroke, or sometimes standing disconsolate by a shallow grave.

Winston Churchill was left behind at the start. The adjutant decided to put him in his place by giving him responsibility for the mess caravan – an imposing name for two donkeys and an overladen mule. 'These are little people,' wrote Churchill of his fellow officers, in a grandiose phrase of which one does not know whether more to deplore the arrogance or admire the perspicacity. 'I can afford to laugh at them. They will live to see the mistake that they have made.' As he trailed a few miles behind his regiment he reflected on the shattered countryside where, 'to the cruelty of man had been added the hostility of Nature'. The desert had indeed extended its sway even over the corridor of cultivated land which had once fringed the Nile. The villages were now abandoned, the fields rank grass and brushwood, the groves of deserted date-palms towered untended over the crumbled huts of the former owners. Here and there a half-starved family of Jaalin Arabs grubbed a precarious living from the soil, every moment glancing furtively over their shoulders lest dervish marauders should swoop suddenly and murderously upon them.

When the steamer carrying the officers of the Grenadier

Guards reached Metemma – the furthest point attained by the relief expedition of 1885 – a stop was made to visit the ghosts of the past and recall the moment when the news came to the advancing army that Khartoum had fallen and Gordon was dead. George Jeffreys had been a boy just going to Eton when Khartoum fell. He went ashore at Metemma in the spirit of an idle sight-seer but returned aboard an embittered veteran, for Mahmud's army had ravaged the village on the way north. 'The place is thick with skulls and bones,' he noted in his diary, 'and many corpses are practically complete, having dried to a kind of mummies in the sun. There must be several thousand of them lying about and the vultures still seem to find plenty of occupation.'

Nor were such atrocities things of the past. Beatty had aboard his gun-boat Charles Fergusson, a Grenadier Guards officer now second in command of the Xth Sudanese and a Scotsman from the great Ayrshire house of Kilkerran. They stopped by a ravaged village. Out stumbled an Arab, almost literally holding his head on with his hands; a savage blow from the sword of a Baggara horseman had cut so deeply into the base of his neck. Beatty and Fergusson had no medical training, but a British officer, they reckoned, should be ready for any eventuality. The wound was first disinfected with Beatty's carbolic toothpaste. They then discovered a ball of thick red twine of a kind used for mending sails. Beatty held the head in place while Fergusson sewed it on with a heavy sail-needle. Incredibly the man survived and at subsequent meetings always greeted Fergusson as his saviour. His head, however, was noticeably crooked. Beatty blamed Fergusson's performance with the needle; Fergusson claimed that Beatty had failed to hold the head on straight.

Kitchener and Wingate review their troops

And so the army came to Wad Hamed. Normally it was a peaceful, even idyllic spot. The broad Nile at this point was thickly set with islands, luxuriantly green; 'like the Thames above Pangbourne', was the prosaic phrase of the Methodist chaplain. On the bank of the river itself a grove of palms waved lazily in the evening breeze. But now the pastoral stillness was shattered. The camp sprawled for two miles along the river, protected to the north by a deep canal and on the other two landward sides by a palisade of thorn bushes staked down to form a zariba. Across the wide area thus encompassed were laid out the grass huts and blanket tents of the Egyptian and Sudanese and the white tents of the British Brigade. The tents were enjoying their last outing for henceforth the army would march in battle order and all such luxuries, like the fresh bread baked each morning by the Service Corps and the soda water sold by the enterprising Greek trader, would be dispensed with. On a knoll overlooking it all stood the Sirdar's white pavilion, a high staff standing

Advance of the First Brigade from Wad Hamed

in front of it from which flew the red flag of Egypt. And along the normally deserted riverside clustered a forest of masts, sails and funnels; a fleet of gun-boats and steamers, barges and *gyassas*. A town, a port, a dockyard had sprung up almost overnight, to vanish again with equal speed as soon as they had served their purpose.

On August 21 all the troops at Wad Hamed – which, except for a small rearguard, was in effect the entire expeditionary force – marched three miles out into the desert for an inspection by the Sirdar. It was the first time that the army had assembled. Eight thousand two hundred British troops; 17,600 Egyptians and Sudanese; 44 field guns and 20 maxims on land, 36 guns and 24 maxims on the water; 2470 horses, 5250 camels, 230 donkeys: this was the force that was to march on Omdurman. As it lined up in the burning sun, 1260 miles from Cairo and only a mere sixty from its destination, the army for the first time conceived itself as a unity, as the sum of its disparate parts drawn from such different races and regions.

When Kitchener rode out on his inevitable white charger to inspect the troops, it was a solemn moment, solemn enough to impress even the normally acerbic and irreverent Major Bagot. 'It was a fine thing to see the Sirdar setting his army in array, and when he cantered down the line, very erect in his saddle, with the eye of a hawk, and looking every inch a great commander, it was a stirring thing.'

Two days later the gun-boat *Melik* pulled in beside the Jebel Royan, a steep, rocky hill normally to the east of the Nile but at high water turned into an island. An advance supply depot had been established there to service the army in its march. 'Monkey' Gordon, *Melik*'s commander, took his telescope and scrambled to the highest peak. Dust and heat-haze made it hard to see but surely there, some forty miles to the south, was the blurred outline of a great city? And that fleck of white in the centre, which through the telescope seemed to be a building, square and domed; must not that be the Mahdi's tomb? It was fitting that the nephew of General Gordon should be the first member of the expeditionary force to catch a glimpse of Omdurman.

CHAPTER IV

'There will be a Battle'

OMDURMAN – the name is like the groan of a great gong
rolling mournfully across the desert; a sound redolent of
all the mystery of Arabia; of shadowy lattice-work in
still, secretive courtyards; of ancient temples; of great
markets where the camel caravans brought in the scents
and silks of China and Circassian slave girls exhibited
their charms before the lustful sheikhs. Reality, alas, was
less romantic. It is hard to believe that any city can have
had less charm, less dignity, less distinction than this
squalid accretion of mud hovels and straw-walled huts.

At the time Gordon died Omdurman had been no more
than a large village, sheltering a few fishermen and the
occasional bandit. When the Mahdi abandoned Khartoum
to make his capital on the other side of the Nile he intended
the new site to be no more than a temporary camping
ground on the way to Cairo, Damascus or some yet more
glorious destiny. Omdurman, therefore, grew without
thought for posterity – not that either the craftsmen or the
money were available to make it architecturally more
imposing, even if the will had been there. The Khalifa had
less illusions than his former master about his destiny as
ruler of a pan-Arabian empire but, even though he
accepted that Omdurman would probably be his capital
for life, he did little to embellish the squalid sprawl which
he inherited. On the contrary, he vastly aggravated the
unpleasantness of the city by his policy of centralisation,
compelling far-flung tribes to leave the desert and help
swell the dingy slums. By 1898 the capital sprawled for
nearly six miles along the bank of the Nile and, at its

largest, extended almost three miles inland from the river. One concession was made to the principles of town-planning, but exclusively for military reasons: a few wide avenues were driven through the endless slums so that the Khalifa's bodyguard could rapidly reach any part of the city which threatened insurrection.

The Khalifa was responsible for one building with some pretensions to the monumental. It was the Mahdi's tomb; the same white patch that Monkey Gordon had seen from the peak of the Jebel Royan. Though the tallest building in the Sudan, the tomb was unsensational by other standards: a square white building, thirty feet high and thirty-six feet along each wall, surmounted by a hexagonal block rising another fifteen feet, and crowned by a dome forty feet high. Above the apex of the dome were three hollow brass balls, one mounted above the other, and topmost of all a lance pointed towards the sky. Slatin suggested that this symbolised the Khalifa's intention to wage war even against the heavens if his wishes were not carried out. He can hardly be proved wrong but it is difficult to credit that a man who made war so vociferously in the name of Allah could have harboured, or at least expressed, a thought of such impiety. This modest structure seemed to the inhabitants to be not only a miracle of modern engineering but also, as the repository of the sacred relics, a place of singular holiness and religious significance. Legends rapidly grew up around it: it was commonly believed that a *djinn* had lent a hand from time to time while the building was going on, and no one doubted that it would defy the attacks of any infidel invader.

The tomb was the spiritual centre of the city. Immediately adjoining it was the Great Mosque: great in name though strikingly unimpressive to the outward or occidental eye. It was indeed no more than a large unpaved compound, in one corner of which a galvanised iron shed,

EGYPTIAN CAVALRY (Summer Kit).

EGYPTIAN INFANTRY.   BRITISH OFFICER OF

Winter.   Summer.

SE (Khaki' Kit). SOUDANESE INFANTRY.

Coloured lithograph by R. Simkin

the mosque itself, looked vaguely ill at ease, as if transplanted there from some builder's yard in a London suburb. Clustered around the mosque were a few brick buildings, none large and only one, the Khalifa's palace, boasting a second storey. Nowhere in the city would connoisseurs of the exotic have met with a sadder disappointment. The peak of luxury, proudest jewel of this desert paradise, was a brass bed. The Khalifa's bath also had two brass taps; not, of course, taps connected to any source of water but still in all probability the only taps of the kind to be found in the Sudan. Several of the rooms had carpets and there were cushions everywhere. Such was the extent of the palatial glories. Only in the adjoining hareem, where some 400 wives attended by a regiment of eunuchs awaited the Khalifa's pleasure, was anything to be found which would have seemed out of place in the mean house of some small-time Cairo merchant.

Though the Khalifa's palace was the most imposing of the brick buildings around the mosque, the house of his son, Osman Sheikh el Din was more lavish in its furnishings. Osman was something of a sybarite, even perhaps had grown a little soft. He had earned the disapproval of his father and the more bellicose of the emirs by arguing that negotiations should be opened with the invaders and some sort of settlement arrived at. His sins had now been forgiven and he was back in his father's favour, but he was still a suspect figure to certain of the dervish leaders. His style of life did nothing to appease them. His prime extravagance was a large garden, the most striking evidence of his love of luxury a pair of heavy brass chandeliers looted from the palace at Khartoum; but even such mundane trappings seemed dreadful to puritans like Ali Wad Helu, who had once been accepted as heir apparent to the Mahdi himself and still enjoyed a prestige exceeded by nobody except the Khalifa.

Around this inner core of the city, protecting and isolating it from all lesser mortals, lay a great stone wall, four feet thick and fourteen feet high, running for nearly three quarters of a mile along the bank of the Nile, then snaking inland to encircle tomb, mosque, palace and most of the other principal buildings. Architecturally the wall was the most striking feature of the city; symbolically its significance was still greater. The Khalifa was a man who lived in terror; terror not of the infidels, whom he was confident he could destroy, but of his own compatriots, whom he had overcome by guile and kept in subjection by ruthless repression. He feared poison, he feared the assassin's knife; he feared his potential rivals, his alleged supporters, even his own family. Within his wall he skulked nervously, venturing rarely into the outer city and almost never beyond the confines of Omdurman itself. His huge bodyguard, drawn from his own Taiasha tribe and nearly two thousand strong, thronged always close around him, sealing off every approach to his palace and ensuring that everyone who sought an audience with him – even Osman Digna or Ali Wad Helu himself – left his sword and knife in the ante-room and approached his ruler discreetly disarmed.

Ever since Mahmud's army had been destroyed at the Atbara, the Khalifa had been convinced that the final stand must be made in or near Omdurman. In this he was supported by his son, Sheikh el Din, as well as by the prudent Osman Digna. The latter, indeed, left to himself would probably have abandoned the city altogether and retreated ever further up the Nile, drawing on the invaders behind him until their communications were stretched to breaking point and their morale began to crumble under the searing sun. Strategically this might have been the wisest course, indeed several of the British commanders were certain it would be adopted, but Slatin insisted that the Khalifa could never desert his capital and the tomb of the Mahdi without losing the support of his people. Slatin was proved right. Whatever the Khalifa's inclinations, it is unlikely that the champions of a more aggressive and forward policy, Osman Azrak and Ali Wad Helu in particular, would ever have submitted to so abject a surrender. On the contrary they urged that the Khalifa should sally out with all his army and confront the infidels as far to the north as possible. Not a foot of the sacred soil should be given up unnecessarily.

At first it seemed that the counsels of the bellicose had been heeded. The Khalifa agreed that seven forts should be built around the Shabluka Gorge at the Sixth Cataract – the point at which Captain Rawlinson and the Rifle Brigade had had so uncomfortable a passage. These forts dominated the river and the fire that could have been directed from them at passing traffic would have made it impossible even for the heavily armoured gun-boats to advance. From the landward side, too, the forts were in a strong position and could have offered a stout defence against any attack by Kitchener's soldiers. Yet Kitchener would not have been able to by-pass the position and continue towards Omdurman since to do so would 'have been to sacrifice his gun-boat support and lose touch with his river-borne supplies.

The forts were duly built and occupied. Then came a change of heart. The Khalifa had dreamed a dream. The enemy were to be destroyed on the plains of Kerreri, only a few miles from the city. It would be disrespectful to Allah to seek to oppose them elsewhere. More cogently, except to the eye of the visionary, it would be disastrous for morale if, only a few months after Mahmud's disaster at the Atbara, another dervish force were cut off and destroyed piecemeal. Osman Azrak and Ali Wad Helu can hardly have been convinced by this reasoning but when the Khalifa had made up his mind there was no room for further argument. The forts were abandoned, the British boats passed the Sixth Cataract without more hindrance than that offered by nature.

Now came the question of exactly where the final battle should be fought. Some six miles north of Omdurman the Kerreri hills ran almost from the village of the same name on the banks of the Nile to a point four miles or so inland. They could be outflanked, but only by an arduous detour over difficult country. If a stand was to be made outside the city, then this was the obvious place. Would it be better to confront the invaders in defensive positions dug into the hills, or await their coming in the city itself and destroy them in the maze of streets? This latter course would cost the lives of many civilians but, in Omdurman, every house would be a deadly trap and the fearful power of the British artillery could not be brought to bear. The debate dragged on but, once again, the Khalifa had made up his mind and it was the Khalifa alone who would decide. Some small part of the army might be permitted to welcome the infidels on the plains but the real battle would be fought out in the streets of Omdurman. It was a conclusion which would have filled Kitchener with dismay if word of it had filtered through to his headquarters as he urged the army on to its final march.

But the dervishes did not intend to sit passively and await the arrival of the enemy. The threat of the gunboats caused more concern in Omdurman than any other element in the allied army, and the energies of the dervishes were devoted to ways of blocking the Nile against them. An ambitious plan was devised for sealing off the river shortly below the point in front of Khartoum at which it divided into the Blue Nile and the White Nile. A series of buoys was to stretch across the river, linked by a heavy chain. The weight of the chain would draw the buoys just below the surface so that the unsuspecting gunboats would find their paddles and propellers inextricably entangled and would be a helpless prey for the boarding parties which would swoop down on them from the bank. The device was primitive, but might have proved effective. Unfortunately for the Sudanese, however, the Khalifa entrusted the task to Mahommad Burrai, a former employee of Gordon in the arsenal at Khartoum. Burrai hated Mahdism with a concentrated fury which had built up over fourteen years. Here at last was his chance of revenge. The task was immaculately carried out except that certain of the buoys were not properly tethered. The current swept them to the centre of the river, whereupon the chain snapped and rattled to the bottom. When the Khalifa ordered Burrai to try again it was found that not enough chain was left to replace the lengths sunk deep in the Nilotic mud.

A more sophisticated method was now adopted. Two large tubular boilers had been rusting in the dockyard at Khartoum ever since the fall of the town. These were to be stuffed with explosive and rigged up with an electrical connection so that they could be set off from the bank when the enemy boat was above it. Again the job was given to Burrai. This time he appealed for advice to Charles Neufeld, the German engineer, who had been the Khalifa's prisoner for thirteen years. When the old paddle boat, the *Ismailia*, put out with the mine lashed to its side, he took with him instructions for cutting the wires and so making the explosives harmless. Something went wrong. Whether Burrai chose the wrong wire or the ramshackle device was anyhow hopelessly insecure, the result of his action was to explode the mine and blow the *Ismailia* to matchwood. The unfortunate saboteur was severely wounded and died a week later.

Undeterred, the Khalifa tried again. The second boiler was filled with explosive and carried to the centre of the Nile. Reverently it was lowered to the river bed and the electrical connections fitted up. The new engineer, however, was a prudent man. He had no idea what had gone wrong in the previous operation but the results had clearly been disagreeable for the participants. He did not intend to court a similar fate and so took the precaution of rendering the explosive harmless before he immersed it in the river. Then he proudly reported that the mine was laid. Only when Beatty in the *Fateh* sailed unscathed over the danger area did the discomfited dervishes realise that modern science had betrayed them once again.

Meanwhile hectic mobilisation went on all over the Sudan. The leading emirs were despatched to their tribal areas to recruit every man fit to carry arms and rally them at Omdurman. The ultimate proof of serious purpose was that no women were allowed to accompany their menfolk, 'not even a slave-girl or a concubine'. Most of the warriors who answered the call were fanatical enough in their support of Mahdism but there were dissidents and sceptics even among the ranks of the faithful. Babikr Bedri was a young intellectual who was to survive until the age of ninety-four and make a great contribution to the education of his people. He viewed the Khalifa's cause with cool detachment and the prospect of dying for it with undisguised distaste. A family friend called Rajab al-Makk, who was a fervent member of the Khalifa's guard, came to the house and told how he had heard Abdullahi himself declare that the Turks would reach Kerreri on September 3 and be destroyed within the next forty-eight hours. 'I waggled my ears with my hands in the way that boys do when they want to show that what has been said is a lie, and Rajab said, "Babikr! Do you mean that I am a liar or the Khalifa?" ' Bedri was saved from having to reply by another friend who broke in, saying that they all felt the same thing but had been slower in showing their doubts. 'You're a faithless bunch of hypocrites!' cried Rajab, and stormed from the house.

Even the Khalifa seemed to have qualms. He frequently

quoted the Mahdi as having predicted victory at Kerreri but now began to search for someone who had actually heard these comforting words. No one came forward; indeed one sage cast doubt on the very possibility that the Mahdi might have spoken in this way. The Khalifa contrived to cherish his illusions but not all his followers proved so gullible. Babikr Bedri's father was one of the least sanguine. Often, his son recorded, he used to say:

'I'm always thinking about the Khalifa's army and the government army; I believe they'll meet at Kerreri, and after a bit I see the Khalifa and his army going pitter-pat to Omdurman, running away from the government army. I can see no victory for them at all.'

Shortly after the river had been mined a parade was held in front of the Mahdi's tomb. A ritual habitually indulged in during such ceremonials was for one of the more eminent emirs to charge directly towards his men, pull up violently a few feet away from them, shake his spear triumphantly above his head and then gallop off to left or right. Ali Wad Helu was carrying out this manoeuvre with his usual brio when his horse slipped, dashing itself and its master into the front row of the startled troops. Six Arabs were carried off with serious injuries, the horse was lamed and Ali Wad Helu himself broke his wrist.

For anyone undertaking a new enterprise to fall from a horse was one of the worst of omens. Black dismay struck the troops while the Khalifa retreated hurriedly into the Mahdi's tomb. He was to remain there in urgent consultation with his former master for the next eight days. The dervish army was aghast: only Sheikh el Din, jealous both of Ali Wad Helu's horsemanship and his renown as a warrior, saw something to rejoice at in the disaster.

Meanwhile the British army, though demoralised by no such unpropitious portent, was not in a particularly cheerful mood. The great march forward from Wad Hamed was proving a protracted and painful business and there was no confidence among the rank and file that it would lead to anything in the end. Every hill they came to was undefended, every village deserted, was it not probable that so it would go on, that they would pursue their elusive foe to the furthest confines of Nubia and beyond without ever coming to grips with them?

The final advance began on August 24 when two Sudanese and three Egyptian brigades set out for the next camp opposite the Jebel Royan. With them went the 7th Squadron of the Egyptian cavalry under the command of Captain Douglas Haig, an intensely ambitious cavalry officer of thirty-eight. Haig had studied at Brasenose under Dr Cradock, a sporting Principal whose traditional address to freshmen was: 'Ride, sir, ride – I like to see the gentlemen of Brasenose in top boots.' Haig duly rode, indeed played polo for England, but such diversions could not distract him from a dourly professional pursuit of advancement in his career. Now he was poised for quick promotion and ever conscious of the fact that he was far better at his job than many officers senior to him. This conviction of superiority was to remain with him until eventually it was rewarded by a field-marshal's baton. Now he was in charge of the advance guard. Kitchener intended to stagger this phase of the march over three or four days, despatching a different section of the infantry each day and allowing it to bivouac where it pleased along the way. Only on the next stage, when they left the Jebel Royan camp, would the army march as a single unit.

A casual glance at the map, showing Jebel Royan a mere seven miles as the crow flew from Wad Hamed, would suggest that even the most unseasoned infantry would need no more than a day to cover the distance. In the flat plains of the Sudan that deceitful cicerone, the crow, is not as wholly irrelevant to the realities of travel as in most other parts of the world, but here no troops could hope to emulate its example. To pass the mountains around the Shabluka gorge a vast detour was necessary and even then the army found itself scrabbling up harsh slopes in a temperature of $110°$ or $115°$ in the shade.

The Lincolnshires marched on the third day, August 26. They bivouacked in a good shady camp and were off before dawn on the second leg of the march with the comfortable feeling that the worst was behind them. For Lt Hodgson, the younger son of a Lincolnshire squire who had never before travelled far from home, everything seemed new and exciting. The next twelve hours went far to change his mind. The going was bad from the start and, by the time the sun was fully up and the heat intense, the battalion was fighting its way uphill. 'Loose stones and sharp flints which slashed through the soles of boots, constant dry water courses, tussocks of rough grass, stunted mimosa and other thorny bushes, interspersed with between 300 yds and a mile of loose shingle,' did nothing to make progress more agreeable. More and more men were dropping out, water in the bottles was running low and when they fell in after their third halt morale in the ranks of the Lincolnshires had reached a dismally low ebb. Then the word ran around that from now on it was downhill all the way. The pace quickened, the drums began to play, there was cheering and applause after every tune, and the regiment marched into camp with spirits almost as high as when they had left Wad Hamed. The euphoria did not last long however. At the last moment General Gatacre changed all the arrangements for the layout of the camp so that the luckless troops were kept marching up and down while new areas were arranged. 'He is the most impossible man,' grumbled Bagot. 'Does everyone else's work and lets brigadiers do nothing and Lyttelton does not seem man enough to stand up for his rights.'

The 21st Lancers brought up the rearguard with what

remained of the Egyptian cavalry, the Camel Corps and the battery of Horse Artillery. Mounted or not, it was no easy march to cover in a day. 'A gross piece of mismanagement and miscalculation on the part of the Sirdar,' stormed Churchill. 'We kill five or six horses every day. It reveals an amount of folly and wicked waste of public money hardly credible.' 'The 21st eat like pigs,' this irascible subaltern continued, 'we get nothing to eat but bully-beef, biscuits and warm beer. Arrangements for march guard and convoy duty are lamentable and a vigorous enemy would make hay of all of us.' It was not to be the only time in his career that Winston Churchill was to find himself the only person around who appeared to know his job.

The last units trickled into camp on the night of August 27. The missing contingent of the Rifle Brigade debouched from its steamer, eager to tell of the horrors of the Sixth Cataract and vaguely aggrieved that everyone else seemed more concerned to describe the tribulations which *they* had suffered on dry land. Sunday, August 28 was to be the day on which the whole force resumed the march but in 1898 Sunday was still Sunday and everything stopped for church parade. The Rev. A. W. Watson preached an excellent sermon, the service concluded, but before the men could break away the busy figure of the Divisional Commander strode out to confront them. 'Gatacre also got on his legs and addressed us;' commented Hodgson disrespectfully, 'but as he turned himself entirely to the Guards and what was heard was twaddle no one was sorry when he finished.'

The Lincolnshires, it seems, were lucky to be denied the benefit of the general's words. '. . . one of the most foolish and insulting speeches a man could make,' was one summary, while Colonel Martin, no mean artist himself when it came to being offensive, was almost beside himself with indignation. So far no one, said the general, had done

73

anything worth speaking of. Morale was bad and training worse. The officers did not know how to look after their men and the men lacked the guts to march. Heaven help them, and England, if they showed the same spirit in battle. And after it was all over. . . ? 'I suppose the Egyptian Government will give you a medal; and what for? For nothing! And I suppose the British Government will give you a second medal – for nothing!'

Not unduly put out by this diatribe, the army marched at 4 p.m. Now for the first time it could be seen arrayed in its full majesty. The advance was made on a broad front, which could swing almost immediately into battle formation if need arose. The left flank rested most of the time on or near the Nile. Because of the thick scrub which fringed the river and in which enemies could lurk unseen, this was deemed to be the danger point. Usually it was occupied by the First British Brigade with Brigadier Wauchope of the Black Watch on a white pony at its head. Then, stretching for a mile or more into the desert, dressed with extraordinary precision considering the roughness of the ground, lay the great span of the expeditionary force: the Egyptians, with a green flag for each battalion and a rich diversity of minor standards to the taste of every company commander; the Grenadiers, with their ensign carried by the Queen's Company; the Seaforths, bearing a yellow banner boasting *Cuidich n Righ*, 'I serve the King'; the Union Jack over the divisional staff, still tattered from the bullets of Mahmud's soldiers at the Atbara; the drums and bagpipes perpetually urging on the men to fresh endeavour. In front of all rode the Sirdar with his chief of staff at his side. ''e looks as if 'e means business, and it ud take a dozen nigger Khalifas to get the best of 'im,' a private in the Warwickshires was quoted as observing. The sentiment sounds a little too edifying to ring entirely true but, whatever his vices and his limitations, no one ever questioned Kitchener's capacity for inspiring

74

confidence in the men he commanded.

But still the doubt whether the Khalifa would be obliging enough to wait for Kitchener's arrival hung over the advancing host. The 21st Lancers, indignant that the Egyptian cavalry was being preferred to them for reconnaissance work, saw all hope of action disappearing. Colonel Martin even nerved himself to protest to the Sirdar. Drily Kitchener assured him that there would be work for his regiment to do in the not too distant future. For the Second Brigade, who had so recently arrived in the Sudan and had never even seen a dervish, the whole expedition took on a feverish unreality. What possibility was there that in this vast continent an enemy would assemble in sufficient force to provide a battle? Did the dervishes even exist?

On this last point at least they were soon to have reassurance. On the night of August 28 the army halted at Wadi el Abid and bivouacked behind a rough zariba. At dusk a solitary dervish horseman burst suddenly upon the lines and stopped in consternation. It was difficult to say whether he or the British troops were more surprised. He hurled his spear in a defiant if somewhat ineffective gesture and it plopped harmlessly at the feet of a startled sentry from the Lancashire Fusiliers. A messenger was hurriedly despatched to the commanding officer to enquire whether, in the circumstances, it would be appropriate to open fire. While this point was being debated the dervish, calculating that he had probably out-stayed his welcome, galloped back into the twilight from which he had come. As a military engagement the incident may be felt to lack substance but for many men in the army it was the first tangible proof of the presence of an enemy. As such it was a moment to be cherished.

The army moved ponderously forward. A day was passed at Wadi el Abid, then on the 30th the advance was resumed for a further six miles or so to a place called

Sayol. From there, on the 31st, the army marched in fighting formation on a two brigade front; the British division on the left, the Egyptian army on the right. The cavalry ranged far ahead, penetrating as far as the Kerreri hills and looking down on to the plains in front of Omdurman. Increasingly they encountered evidence of enemy activity: a single horseman, a group of cavalry, finally a patrol seventy strong.

Lt Smyth of the 21st Lancers was up at 3 a.m. and on patrol two hours later. At six that evening he was still hard at it, two miles ahead of the main body of cavalry. 'The bush in front of my Piquet full of Dervish horsemen,' he noted. 'I counted about 100. Eventually about 5.30 they lit a series of bonfires and retired. It was a sign the day's work was over.' A welcome sign, one would imagine. Meanwhile deserters were flocking to join the army; all bearing the same news – the Khalifa with a great army would fight at Omdurman.

Then, on August 30, the Lancers took a prisoner. They swooped on a village of bee-hive shaped straw huts, found it apparently deserted, then lurking in one of the huts discovered a palpable dervish warrior. They searched him and discovered secreted in the folds of his clothes, five Maria Theresa dollars – proof that their prey was a man of substance, possibly an emir. The dollars, his spear and gibbeh were taken as souvenirs and the prisoner marched triumphantly back to camp. He seemed to be trying to communicate with his captors but, since no Lancer spoke a word of Arabic, his efforts were inevitably frustrated. It was noticed, however, that he seemed not so much angry or afraid as bored. The reason was soon discovered. When the Lancers reached the army, Wingate hailed their victim with delight as Eshanni, one of his most valued spies. Eshanni had left Omdurman only thirty hours before and brought much useful news about the dervish army. The Khalifa would fight, he too insisted, and what was more would fight at Kerreri, the plain known to all Mahdists as 'the death place of the infidels'. The Lancers were exhilarated at the prospect but still disgruntled when they had to return their booty to their former prisoner.

Not all Wingate's spies were so fortunate. The following day the body of another of his men was discovered, charred and horribly mutilated, in a captured village. His death, it was only too evident, had been a protracted and not a pleasant one.

With a growing certainty that battle lay ahead the troops marched with fresh enthusiasm. One minor set-back only marred the generally satisfactory picture. The *Zafir*, most powerful of the 1896 class stern-wheel gun-boats and flagship of the whole flotilla, inexplicably sprung a leak as she approached the Shabluka cataract. The ship foundered in a few moments and the officers and crew barely had time to leap clear and scramble to the shore. This was a sad set-back but not a disastrous one. There were still nine gun-boats left, more than enough for the work in hand. Keppel, the commander of the flotilla, transferred his flag to the *Sultan*.

On August 31 the army edged onwards a few more miles to a ridge called Sururab, only six miles short of the Kerreri hills. Speculatively they peered up into the burned brown mass of the mountains. Was the dervish army already concentrated there? Would tomorrow the bleak searing rocks be pitted by bullets and moistened by human blood? It would be a fearful business to fight one's way up those cruel slopes in the face of opposition from a determined enemy. The Egyptian cavalry and the Lancers were sent out to try to find some answers to these questions. Colonel R. G. Broadwood accompanied an advance guard which cantered far off to the right into the foothills. Broadwood was one of the most completely professional soldiers in Kitchener's army. He was a long-legged, lanky,

77

phlegmatic man who had spent so much time on a horse that sometimes he seemed to be more centaur than soldier. Even the censorious Haig in charge of the 7th Squadron admitted that he was 'a very sound fellow . . . excellent at running this show'. Now something caught the eye of a keen-eyed scout, the troop halted, and through a telescope Broadwood made out 'white objects, like tents or camel coverings, flapping in the wind'. The dervishes, it seemed, were there in force.

Meanwhile the Lancers pushed on towards the Kerreri hills themselves. The only sign of life was a vast flock of vultures wheeling lazily overhead. The advancing cavalry looked up with some hostility at these repellent fowls. Was their group, they wondered, being sized up as some sort of *hors d'oeuvre* for the feast to come? And, if so, who was expected to provide the main course? Then, as they neared the hills, signs of more immediately malevolent life appeared. Curious white patches and flecks of colour appeared and were revealed under examination to consist of flags waving in the breeze. It was clearly a dervish camp, though held in what force it was hard to say. Two adventurous young officers rode near it, were fired at and reported that the camp seemed to be lightly held. Their own inclination would no doubt have been to charge in force and thus either confirm the correctness of their judgment or disastrously prove its error. Colonel Martin chose to play a more sober role and withdrew to report. The Sirdar meanwhile, hearing from the gunfire that the Lancers were engaged, sent the gun-boat *Sheikh* up the river in support. Seeing the dervish flags the *Sheikh* opened fire and pumped about thirty shells into the area. The Arab horsemen discreetly retreated to the other side of the hill – if there were casualties among them there was certainly no trace of them to be seen when the Anglo-Egyptian army swept over the hills on the following day. That was the final incident of August 31. The *Sheikh*

78

returned to base while the army settled down on its ridge to enjoy what many people felt was likely to be their last night before the battle. With no serious enemy force this side of the hills they could reasonably hope to enjoy a restful night. So they did – till about 10 p.m. Then came wind, a raw strident wind from the east, and a little later a downpour of torrential rain, rain so heavy that it seemed hardly conceivable in the Sudan. At least it could not last for more than a few moments, and yet, incredibly, it went on for hour after hour. In no time the flimsy blanket shelters had been swamped and the so-called 'waterproof' sheets exposed for the sham they were. One brigadier, finding himself lying in three inches of water, spent the rest of the night peevishly bemoaning his fate in a deck chair. Though he felt his lot to be an unhappy one, to the rest of the army it seemed that only a general officer could expect such luck as to have a deck chair to spend the night in.

Fred Villiers of the *Illustrated London News* was one of a handful of men who somehow still contrived to have their tents with them. He lay gloating mildly over the sufferings of his colleagues and stretched luxuriously in his sleeping bag. Promptly a scorpion bit him. It was as if a red hot skewer had been plunged into his neck and the left side of his body was temporarily paralysed. A servant rubbed ammonia into the wound and whisky, of which he drank almost a whole bottle in the next four hours, did something to dull the pain. It says much for his constitution and his courage that the following day he contrived to keep up with the advancing troops.

'We were a wretched collection of drowned rats as we struggled out of our blankets at reveillé,' wrote Captain Egerton of the Seaforths. 'I know nothing more miserable than parading before daylight in damp khaki-drill, having had precious little sleep and knowing that you will very likely get a bullet in your stomach before midday. . . .

Villiers interviewing Egyptian prisoners

There are occasions when you wonder why you were such a confounded ass as to leave your happy home . . .' John Ewart, another young man on his first active service, was transport officer for the Seaforths. He found that the rain set him some knotty problems. The camels slipped and slithered on the greasy ground, or remained obstinately sprawled on their sides, demonstrating, with patent insincerity, that it was quite impossible for them to find their feet. Even worse, the waterlogged blankets weighed twice as much as they had the night before. 'Never,' commented Ewart sadly, 'has the straw and the camel's back been so vividly before my eyes.'

Grumbling, cursing, stiff and sleepless, the army staggered to its feet, pulled itself together and prepared to march. Then the skies cleared, the sun came out, steam rose from the clammy uniforms, life filtered back to cold, tired bodies. By 9 a.m. the march was well advanced, spirits were high, glory and the dervishes lay ahead. The horrors of the night were soon forgotten; now it was onwards, on to Kerreri, on to Omdurman.

On August 30, from the camp at Sayol, Kitchener had despatched a message to the Khalifa calling on him to surrender. If he did not, the message went on, then Omdurman would be destroyed by bombardment. If the Khalifa wanted to avoid unnecessary bloodshed, then he should at least evacuate women and children from the city under flag of truce. 'Stand firm you and your helpers only in the field of battle to meet the punishment prepared for you by the praised God. But if you and your Emirs incline to surrender . . . we shall treat you with justice and peace.' The note has been cited as evidence of Kitchener's humanity. He can, in fact, hardly have supposed that his ultimatum would be obeyed or even acknowledged. It was not. The Khalifa had emerged refreshed and invigorated from his prolonged colloquy with the Mahdi's ghost. He read the Sirdar's letter with contempt. It came from a *Kafir*, he said, and in a few days he would have all the *Kafirs* in his power. It was not worth a moment's consideration.

The Khalifa was convinced that he had done everything humanly possible to defend his capital and that it was now, to all intents and purposes, impregnable. He had built seventeen new forts: two at Khartoum, two on Tuti Island in the Nile between Khartoum and Omdurman at the point at which the White and Blue Nile separated, two on the east bank opposite Tuti Island and the remaining eleven between the bank of the Nile and the wall of the city. The two on the opposite bank were in jeopardy from Stuart Wortley's advancing Friendlies but the remainder were imposing enough. Within them he had concentrated thirty-two guns, with a further two mounted on steamers and twenty-nine in reserve for use wherever needed in the battle. The guns were, for the most part, ineffective compared with the artillery at the disposal of the Anglo-Egyptian army but they could nevertheless fire projectiles heavy enough to sink a gun-boat.

A waiting game was still the dervishes' prescription for success. The Khalifa saw no reason why he should not sit tight behind his walls and his forts and let the enemy vainly dash themselves to pieces. Then, when they were weakened and demoralised, his army would sally forth and utterly destroy them. The policy was by no means a foolish one and, if persisted in, might have gained a fair measure of success. It made no allowance, however, for the immense superiority of Kitchener's fire power and the damage which the allied guns could do to the dervish defences. It was only to take a few moments bombardment to set the Khalifa wondering how his policy should be revised.

On August 31 he summoned his army to parade on the open plain to the west of Omdurman so that he could hold an inspection and deliver a final harangue. Shortly after dawn the rattle of war drums and the melancholy wail of the ombeya, the Sudanese war-horn fashioned from an elephant's tusk whose sound will echo amazing distances across the desert, announced his departure from the palace. Babikr Bedri was just leaving his house to go to his studies. Hurriedly he handed his papers to his slave and posted off to join the troops. He expected that he would be home the same night but his well-trained slaves were soon on his trail with 'leather jug for ablutions, my prayer-mat, provisions for two days, and apparatus for tea-making (for I could not give up tea . . .)'. It was just as well, for he was not to sleep in his own bed again until after the battle was over.

Meanwhile the Khalifa was making his ceremonial entry on to the parade-ground. First came his escort of armed *mulazemin*, drawn from the most formidable warriors of his own tribe. Then followed six men, each of whom in turn blew the great ombeya which sounded only at the Khalifa's order and in his presence. The buglers, twenty or thirty strong, came next, ready to call advance or retreat at the Khalifa's order. Immediately before the Khalifa came his personal attendants carrying the sacred instruments of his power; the *Rewka*, or leather vessel, in which he would wash before a religious ceremony and the sheepskin prayer carpet on which he alone could kneel. The Khalifa himself rode alone; a little way behind him on one side an Arab, the most trustworthy of all his bodyguard, Ahmed Abu Dukheka, vastly strong and totally fearless, whose privilege it was to lift his master in and out of the saddle; and on the other a negro, chief of the slaves in the royal stable. Finally came the band of about fifty negro slaves who played on antelope horns and drums made from the hollow trunks of trees. To their compatriots, perhaps even to the Arabs, their harmonies seemed sweet, but to the western ear their harsh cacophony sounded at the best grotesque, at the worst totally repellant.

Slowly this picturesque procession wound out on to the parade ground. Awaiting their arrival between fifty and sixty thousand men were drawn up, facing east, their emirs standing a few feet in front of them, a forest of flags rising from their midst. The Khalifa rode once down the lines, then turned to address them. It was a fiery summons to battle; a clarion-call to a *gehad*, a holy war which would sweep the infidels for ever from their land. Some of them would die in battle, he cried, but what could be better than to die in such a cause, what better way to win the love of Allah and to ensure a perpetuity of paradise? For all who fought well there was the promise of unimaginable glory, for any who showed cowardice a lifetime of contempt and an eternity of misery.

As the parade broke up, messengers galloped on to the ground with the news that the invaders had almost reached the Kerreri hills. Tranquilly the Khalifa prepared to make the final dispositions for his inevitable victory.

CHAPTER V

The Day of the Gunboats

SEPTEMBER 1 was the day of the gun-boats; the day in which the Khalifa for the first time suspected that traditional courage and the approval of Allah could avail nothing against the power of modern technology. To the Anglo-Egyptian troops, however, as they squelched wearily away from their camp at Sururab, it seemed as if a tougher and far more primitive form of fighting lay ahead in the distant hills. It was to be some time before the cavalry would report back and, though Kitchener and Wingate were fairly sure that the Kerreri ridge had been deserted and that the engagement would take place on the plains beyond, the rank and file were divided between the pessimists – or perhaps optimists – who foresaw a bloody battle on the upward slopes; and the optimists – or perhaps pessimists – who believed that the dervishes would never stand and fight at all.

Horace Smith-Dorrien of Tresco, in the Scilly Isles, commanding the 13th Sudanese battalion, inclined to the former theory. As one of the only five officers to survive Isandhlwana, by dint of swimming the Buffalo River with a broken arm, clinging to a horse's tail, he had no illusion about the fighting powers of the nigger – as all inhabitants of Africa were designated by the British soldiers, with a fine disregard of creed or colour. 'Sambo (the name given to Sudanese troops) had become more and more cheerful and talkative, and as the Kerreri Ridge was approached, their pace became faster and faster.' He knew his troops would fight enthusiastically if not with noticeable skill; he knew too that in the dervishes they would find an adversary who would tax them to the uttermost.

The fact that it was September 1 lent some piquancy to the advance, at least among those officers addicted to country sports. 'We fully expected to start partridge shooting,' commented Lt Hodgson, though when the Lincolnshires got bogged down in a deep waterlogged khor and fell behind the rest of the advance it seemed that he might miss the start of the season after all. The Guards cheered themselves with the same joke. 'There was a lot of chaff about a wet 1st,' noted Bagot, 'that the turnips would be very wet and the birds wild, and also that Waterloo was on a wet morning.' But when they reached almost to the summit of the ridge and found no opposition, their spirits began to droop. The Guards crested the hill at about 10.30 a.m. Visibility was still poor and the plains ahead seemed to be filled only by a vast swirling emptiness. Had they come all this way in search of a will-o-the-wisp? 'There won't be no bleeding fight,' expostulated one angry guardsman. 'They ain't got it in 'em. Bleeding cowards, that's what they are!'

The cavalry had already proved him wrong. The Lancers, on the left, kept close to the river and at first saw little except the long line of gun-boats steaming resolutely at 300 yards intervals towards the enemy. The inevitable escort of vultures was surveying them from on high or descending and waddling by the side of the horses so as to take a closer look. Broadwood, meanwhile, took the Egyptian cavalry in a wide arc over the tip of the Kerreri hills and round the flank to their right. They were the first to look down on what was to be the battlefield. The haze was thick enough to limit the view but it could still be seen that a rolling sandy plain, striped with the occasional watercourse, dotted with stray mimosa bushes, but still basically flat and featureless, was all that stood between them and Omdurman. One solitary hill, the Jebel Surgham, reared abruptly from the desert about three quarters of a mile from the Nile and half way between the Kerreri hills and the city. From it a sandy ridge ran north-west into the desert, so that a large area of ground between the Jebel Surgham and Omdurman was hidden from the watchers on the Kerreri hills. The broad, grey Nile unrolled majestically to the left of the panorama with the scruffy mud village of Egeiga sprawled messily along its bank.

The plain seemed deserted but Broadwood quickly gave the order to advance to the next ridge. This was likely to be the decisive moment. He knew that what he saw from the Jebel Surgham could well foreshadow the pattern of the battle. If there were no dervishes in view then this would probably mean that the Khalifa would have to be winkled painfully out of the city or, worse still, had fled from the area altogether. Broadwood cantered across the intervening patch of desert, Steevens of the *Daily Mail* keeping as close behind him as protocol permitted. The forest of mud huts was clear in the distance about three miles away but it was at first hard to be sure exactly what it was which they could glimpse in the slight mist that still hung about the Khor Shambat, the watercourse which drained the plain about half a mile from the city. There seemed to be a long white line; was it banners or tents? Both perhaps? And then, in front of it, gradually becoming clearer, a longer, thicker line of black. A barricade of thorn-bushes? A broad trench? Suddenly the line seemed to sway, to move forward, and the watchers could see that it was made up of men, a dense wall of men poised to roll forward like some irresistible ocean. There could be no more room for doubt. The dervish army would stand and fight rather than surrender its cherished city.

Churchill, away on the left with the 21st Lancers, who could now see the same spectacle from a vantage point near the river, assumed that the whole of the Khalifa's army was already ranged before his eyes. Accurate infor-

Winston Churchill as Second Lieutenant

mation about the dervish dispositions is hard to come by but it in fact seems most likely that only the Jehadin and Mulazemin under Sheikh el Din were at that moment outside the city. This was a massive force, more than 30,000 strong, but it was far from being the cream of the dervish army. The reason, indeed, that it was where it was rather than with the Khalifa and the rest of the army within the walls of Omdurman, was that morale was so low among the tribes that it was feared there would be mass desertions if a chance was given. The Khalifa had left instructions that a picked band of warriors was to search the city three hours after dusk and slit the throat of any man able to carry arms who was found skulking in his house.

The precaution was no doubt necessary but it led to one unfortunate result. Much of the arms and ammunition in the Khalifa's arsenal was to be distributed at the last moment so as to ensure that it was used on the infidels rather than expended on less meritorious vendettas between rival factions or families within the dervish ranks. The last moment came and the army was miles away in the open desert. The rifles lay inactive in the armoury while more than half Sheikh el Din's soldiers marched into battle with only their spears and their courage to pit against the Gatlings and howitzers of the Sirdar's army. Nor did the manoeuvre serve its purpose. That night as Neufeld lay chained in the Khalifa's prison he could hear the pat, pat, of naked feet slipping through the city away from the future battlefield. Could these be fugitives; or was the Khalifa shifting his forces to face some new and unexpected threat? Next day Sheikh el Din knew the answer when he found that nearly 6,000 of his troops had fled under cover of darkness.

As the dervish army peered suspiciously across the miles of sand and stone at the enemy cavalry who were now lined up on the distant ridge, a riderless horse, head down, trudged slowly across the lines towards them. Presumably some unfortunate from the Egyptian cavalry had lost his mount. To the watchers, however, it seemed a fearful portent. The day before, the Khalifa had told them of his vision in which he had seen the Prophet riding on his mare at the head of a host of avenging angels. Now the prophecy seemed to have been stood upon its head. The incident was a fresh cause for dismay, a new incentive to the less belligerent to say goodbye to the battlefield before it was too late.

It was probably the alarm caused by this otherwise trifling incident and the bad effects on his men of seeing the enemy cavalry roaming with impunity under their very noses that led Sheikh el Din to order an advance. To the rhythm of the war drums the line swept forward, a black stain seeping across the rusty grey of the desert surface. 'It was not the whole of their army which advanced, nor did they mean to attack us,' judged Captain Sparks, an ex-ranker veteran of the 3rd Egyptian Brigade, and there can be little doubt that he was right. At the most the Sheikh hoped to cut off a few units of the Egyptian cavalry. To the thin line of cavalry, however, the advance looked imposing enough, and there seemed no reason to doubt that it would continue until it ended in a head-on collision with the Anglo-Egyptian army now scrambling through the Kerreri hills. Messengers were sent hastening to warn Kitchener of what was coming and the cavalry began to pick their way prudently back from their exposed position. By the time the advancing dervishes crested the ridge which Broadwood had recently occupied, only a mile separated the two bodies; the dervish swords were clearly visible, glinting in the now brilliant sunlight.

Meanwhile, on the other bank of the Nile, Stuart Wortley and his irregulars had advanced from village to village; calling in the gun-boats whenever the resistance seemed inconveniently stubborn. There had been several sharp skirmishes, but always the dervishes had disengaged at the last minute. Finally, early in the morning of September 1, they came to a village south of Halfaya and almost opposite the point where the Khor Shambat debouched into the Nile. If the Mahdists were to make a stand anywhere it had to be here. It quickly appeared that the dervish leaders saw the need for resistance quite as clearly as Wortley and his men. The enemy were in force within the scruffy buildings of the village and showed no signs of yielding ground.

Wortley first threw in a contingent belonging to the Gimiab tribe but these showed some reluctance to play the role of shock-troops which had been so optimistically allotted them. Instead they halted and performed a war dance which, while no doubt disconcerting to the oppo-

The gunboat 'Fattha' commanded by Lieutenant Beatty

sition, failed to bring them quickly to the point of surrender. Wortley therefore called upon his most stalwart
fighting men, the Jaalin tribesmen. These had been carefully trained in the use of the Remington rifle but now
that battle was upon them the need for such sophisticated
devices temporarily escaped them. They fired once into
the air, calling on Allah to direct the bullets, then joyfully
flung the rifles away and went into the fight with broad-
bladed spears. From house to house they hacked the enemy.
Sixty-five of them were killed but when they had finished
350 dervishes lay dead, including Isa Zachnieh, a cousin
of the Khalifa. No prisoners were taken; Wortley Mon-
tagu did his best to ensure that those who wished to surrender were given the opportunity, but his men had old
scores to settle and his best was not good enough. It was
not the first or the last time in the campaign that butchery
of this kind occurred.

Resistance had hardly ended before the boats were alongside with the howitzers on board. Major F. B. Elmslie was in command of the 37th Field Battery of the Royal Artillery. He was aghast when he saw the state of the bank, deep soft mud in which the men floundered and which was soon smeared over the ropes, making them almost too slippery to pull on. Somehow the guns were hauled ashore and set up. The Battery had been training for months for this operation, hurling their missiles at a replica of the walls of Omdurman. It was the first time that high explosive shells had ever been used by troops in the field but there was not one premature explosion or other accident. Each shell weighed fifty pounds, with a bursting charge of five pounds of Lyddite. They roared through the air with the ferocity of an express train going under a bridge and had shown in practice that they could blast holes a foot deep in the stoutest stone and pile up a mountain of rubble for the attacking infantry to scale. Their role today, however, was not only to breach the wall but to make the centre of the city so hot that the Khalifa would not dare to choose it as the site for his final stand. As Colonel a'Court, Brigade Major to Lyttelton with the 2nd British Brigade and later to win fame as a war correspondent under the name of Repington, put it in another of those sporting metaphors so dear to the British officer, the howitzers 'played the part of the terrier and induced Reynard to come out of his earth'.

Long before the terrier had got to work the gun-boats had begun to play their part. Crouching in their recently constructed forts, confident in the powers of rubble, Nilotic mud and the strong shield of Allah to protect them against the missiles of the infidel, the dervishes had no doubt that they could easily drive off their attackers. Their first disappointment came when the gun-boats glided easily over the mine which should have blown one of them at least to smithereens. Then at 11 a.m., when the boats were still out of effective range of the antiquated pop-guns to which the Arabs pinned their hopes, the bombardment began. Beatty commanded the advance flotilla; Hood, who as an Admiral was to go down with his ship at Jutland, acted as second-in-command. The very first shell, which blasted a great hole in the nearest fort and killed its occupants, showed just how easy their task was going to be.

The forts on Tuti Island fought back with particular gallantry and even scored a hit or two, causing minor casualties, but one by one they were challenged and demolished, their ruins sprayed by the deadly Maxim gun. Hopefully the dervish commander in Khartoum telegraphed to the Khalifa in Omdurman to tell him that the attacking gun-boat had been destroyed. A copy of the message lay on the operator's table, to be found after the battle by Captain Ray, the adjutant of the Northumberland Fusiliers. 'Probably if the telegraph clerk had wired the truth,' mused the Captain, 'it would have been "heads off" for him, "heads off" for the man who received the message and "heads off" for the porter who brought it.'

Babikr Bedri heard a sudden burst of fire from the troops around the Khalifa and asked what it was all about. A gun-boat had been sunk, he was told, and another captured; the volley was a victory salute. One of the men present was Madjub Abu Bakr, a relative of Osman Digna. He now began to strike the earth with his long spear; then he stuck it in the rain-wet sand and shouted grandiloquently to Bedri and his companions: 'Hey, you recusants! See the sign of victory.' A few minutes later the firing of the gun-boats died away. Madjub Abu Bakr exulted; 'the veins in the man's throat swelled enormously as he assured us doubters that all the steamers were captured'. But the lull was soon over, the firing resumed. 'Those damned unbelievers have been raised from the dead before the Day of Resurrection,' commented Bedri un-kindly. 'God's curse on them!' The others laughed and poor Madjub 'hung his head in miserable disappointment'.

The gun-boats had now turned their attention to the walls which encompassed the heart of the city. The first few hits seemed to cause comparatively little damage but each blow weakened the structure of the wall and, with a sudden rumble, a large section crumbled to the ground. The guns moved on, battering relentlessly away. Many shells fell harmlessly in open spaces or shattered the houses of luckless civilians but enough struck the wall to breach it in many places. Wherever they landed, a thick cloud of red dust and sand swirled into the air, scarcely to settle before it was blasted back into a fresh maelstrom of violence.

At 1.30 p.m. the howitzers on the east bank joined in the bombardment. Their first target was the Mahdi's tomb; partly because it was the most prominent, almost indeed the only prominent building in Omdurman, but more because the dervishes held it in peculiar reverence. Nothing would more quickly demoralise them than its destruction. 'They were banging away hard,' noted Rawlinson with approval from where he watched on the crest of the Jebel Surgham with Colonel Long, who commanded both the British and the Egyptian artillery in the expeditionary force. Two shells burst near it; then, after a short interval, a third; finally two more in quick succession which en-veloped the whole tomb in an impenetrable cloud. 'When this cleared away,' said Churchill with the cavalry, 'instead of being pointed, it was now flat topped.' There were several more direct hits before the gunners were satisfied that they had sufficiently punctured the divinity that doth hedge a Mahdi; then Elmslie turned his attention to other targets.

His first choice was a barracks on the banks of the Nile. There was one near miss, then a shell landed directly on

93

the roof. 'Inside that barrack must have been the most awful place in the world with the shells bursting there,' he later told an audience of his fellow gunners at Woolwich. 'I saw beams and all sorts of things flying in the air and these fearful explosions were going on. We were firing battery fire at the rate of at least three shots a minute. The great gate of the barrack was facing us on the river bank, and I saw this gate open a bit and men begin to bolt in one's, two's and three's. . . . When one man was bolting a shell happened to burst close to him, and he disappeared altogether; there was no body that I could see.' The fearful results the shells were producing were amply proved when Elmslie sent his second-in-command to inspect the buildings the following day. 'You could see there had been a great deal of effect because there was a lot of dried blood about, and a lot of pieces of men which they had neglected to clean up.' He judged the operation an entire success and the faith put in the powers of Lyddite more than justified: 'The man-killing effects were very good; and I am told the moral effect also was very great.'

To the Khalifa it must have seemed that the bombardment might continue until his whole city was destroyed. His men were already appalled by the havoc which had been done around their sacred tomb.

'When the huge crack appeared in the dome of the tomb,' wrote Babikr Bedri, 'the people were dumbfounded; their shouting ceased, even the neighing of the horses was stilled, and at the sunset prayer I could not hear the first "God is the most great" from the leader.' With his men in such a mood the Khalifa felt that to continue to keep them in the centre of the city, dolefully surveying the ruin of their temple and exposed to constant danger from the bombardment, would surely be disastrous. A quick change of plan was agreed to and the dervish army, reinforced by every able-bodied man on whom the press-gangs could lay their hands, surged towards the plain out-

94

side the city. With their removal vanished the Khalifa's best chance; that of involving the enemy in costly house-to-house fighting in which their superior fire power would be of little service and victory would go to the more obstinate and the more blood-thirsty.

The hot and weary troops now swarming down the south slopes of the Kerreri hills had no idea that the guns were busy winning them this signal advantage. Nor did many of them give the matter a moment's thought. They were more concerned with the searing heat, their exhaustion and near dehydration and the uneasy suspicion that every rock or mimosa bush might shelter a dervish spearman. By midday the bulk of the infantry had converged on the ruined huts of El Egeiga, the little village between the Kerreri Hills and the Nile where they were to draw breath before the next stage of the advance.

As they began to build a zariba of timber and thorn bushes around the village a heliograph flashed frenziedly from the top of the Jebel Surgham, appropriately re-christened for the duration of the battle 'Telegraph Hill'. Samuel Fitzgibbon-Cox, more commonly Fitz-Cox, was in charge of the signal detachment on top of this dominating peak – so far dominating, indeed, that Haig considered the Khalifa's biggest blunder lay in not fortifying it and that Kitchener showed almost equal folly when he failed to garrison it before nightfall. From his eyrie Fitz-Cox could see the whole expanse of the plain before Omdurman. Now he hectically signalled that the dervishes were advancing and fresh forces were swarming out of the city. Kitchener, with a handful of staff officers, had just dismounted. The message was hurriedly transcribed and carried to him where he sat on a clay wall in one of the few patches of shade that the village offered. 'The Sirdar did not budge,' noted Lt Hodgson of the Lincolnshires, 'but sat and ate his lunch and told Fitz to find out what the

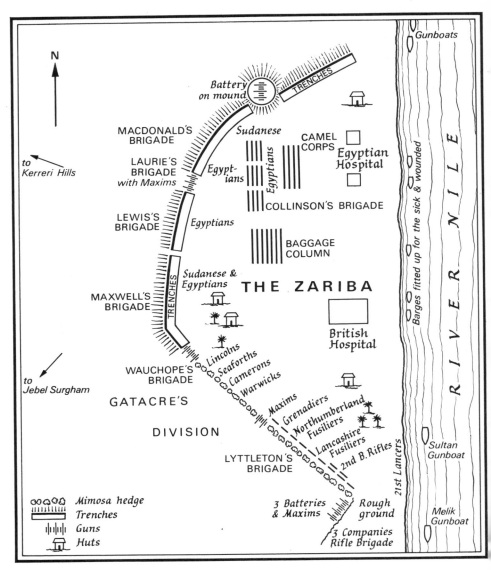

The Zariba before the Battle

Cavalry and the gun-boats were doing. Fitz said he was in a mortal funk lest the sun should go out and stop the helio.' He was probably the only man in the army that day who would not have greeted a few clouds with delighted enthusiasm.

Hodgson, at this stage knowing nothing of the message except that it did not seem to have discomposed the Sirdar, set off for the river with a party to get water, under the comfortable illusion that, short of a battle, the day's work was done. He returned to find chaos once more reigning, with the army abandoning painfully constructed fortifications and marching forward half a mile or so across the desert. In 1898, perhaps even today, few commanders thought to let their rank and file know what was going on. Officers and men alike were baffled by the arcane manoeuvres and tempers were quickly frayed. 'I got very angry with my company,' admitted Bagot, 'as they were not half as quick as in my excitement I had wished them to be ... I forgot that they had practically had nothing to eat and a long march.' What in fact had happened was that Fitz-Cox's message had upset all Kitchener's calculations. He had expected that his army would be able to pass a peaceful if comfortless night at El Egeiga and advance the next day to confront the enemy under the walls of Omdurman or, more probably, in the streets of the city itself. Now suddenly the camping ground bid fair to become a battlefield. 'I expect to be attacked in half an hour,' said Wingate firmly, and when Wingate expected something Kitchener was not slow to act on the assumption that it would take place.

If the army were to fight, it must have room in which to do it. The Sirdar saw that the army's present position did not allow enough room for the reserves to be manoeuvred and the artillery deployed to best advantage. Rawlinson was instructed to reposition the British division on a line at ninety degrees to the river and about half a mile ahead of its present position. He threw forward a flank of about one hundred yards on the extreme left, or river end so that the Rifle Brigade could occupy a small

The gunboat 'Sultan' clearing the banks with Maxim fire

rocky promontory and enfilade any possible attackers. Hardly had they established themselves before Colonel Long rode up and 'declared my pet knoll was the best artillery position in the whole field, and that he wished to place three batteries on it'. So the luckless riflemen found themselves on the move again. The Egyptian and Sudanese battalions were flung round on a wide arc from the end of the British position, so that the final shape of the position was a rough semi-circle with both ends resting on the river.

For two or three hours the men lay around in the midday sun, cursing the stupidity of those in high places. Then, at 3.30 p.m., since their new position was on ground barren even by the standards of the Sudan, they were ordered to return to their former encampment around El Egeiga and drag forward the miscellaneous scraps out of which they had constructed a zariba. The local troops set to work scooping out a shallow trench; the British

The Mahdi's tomb after bombardment by the gunboats

division evidently felt that they would do better to husband
their energies and contented themselves with a few bran-
ches of mimosa as protection not only against a charging
dervish but also against the bullets which would presumably precede him. It was '. . . a very poor thing, as
zaribas go,' commented Ray, 'not from any fault of ours,
but simply because we had got out of the bush, and the
ground all round was open plain from which every stick
had been removed'. Their position established, each regiment sent men out to plant range-finders at appropriate
distances ahead of the line. One officer in the Northumberland Fusiliers even found an old bed in a deserted hut and
placed it at a carefully paced 600 yards from his appreciative
men.

Though the Sirdar was less certain, the rank and file by
now knew that a general advance of the dervishes was
under way and were convinced that a clash was bound
shortly to occur. Eagerly, confidently they awaited the

conflict, half incredulous at their good luck in having the enemy dash themselves against their guns. Morgan Eff Mahmoud, the Adjutant-Major of the 13th Sudanese and a survivor of earlier campaigns against the Mahdi, turned with grim satisfaction to Smith Dorrien. 'If they are such fools as to attack our entrenchment,' he said, 'I shall take tea with the Khalifa tomorrow.' In the Intelligence mess the officers were standing around eating and chatting 'like a race lunch before the big event'. Baron von Tiedemann, the German staff officer who was acting as a kind of floating military attaché with the expedition, was particularly struck by the fact that it was September 1. 'Our great day,' he commented gleefully 'and now your great day: Sedan and Sudan.' Churchill laughed uneasily, unable to decide whether the heavy joke 'cloaked a rather bitter sarcasm'.

Lunch was scarcely over before it was known that the racing was off – for the day at least. The tide of advancing dervishes, now some five miles from the Anglo-Egyptian lines though still cloaked by the ridge running down from the Jebel Surgham, suddenly checked and halted, the whole front instantly immobile as if some voice from heaven had commanded. At a quarter to one, with a rustle that could be heard by the watching cavalry, the Arab soldiers sank to the ground. From his perch at the top of the hill Fitz-Cox watched nervously. Was this no more than a rest? Would the army be on the move again in a few moments? But soon the smoke of cooking fires and the pitching of the occasional tent showed that they were settling down. With a relieved glance towards the still brilliant sun Fitz-Cox turned to his helio and flashed the disappointing news down to the Sirdar.

CHAPTER VI

The Eve of Battle

KITCHENER was now faced with a difficult decision. The traditional dervish tactics were to attack by night, or at least at dawn when the light was still thin and uncertain. They had done this at Tamai and Abu Klea, Khartoum had been stormed at dawn while the garrison still slept, Hicks Pasha had been harried throughout the darkness. It would not be easy at any time to storm the zariba over 3000 yards of open country, but the dervishes would find the task more nearly possible under the cover of night than by brilliant day. On the rough, boulder-strewn ground ten, twenty thousand warriors could creep unseen to within a few yards of the allied sentries. A sudden charge, a few spear thrusts, and they would be into the zariba. In the ferocious hand-to-hand fighting that would follow, the allied superiority in fire power would gain them nothing, their training would count for little: all that would matter would be brute strength and cunning with the sword or spear. 'Lithe and supple,' Neufeld described the dervish soldiers whom he knew so well, 'nimble as cats and as blood-thirsty as a starving man-eating tiger, utterly regardless of their own lives, and capable of continuing stabbing and jabbing with spear and sword while carrying half a dozen wounds, any one of which would have put a European *hors de combat*.' If the Egyptian troops panicked and broke, the Sudanese and British might find themselves assailed from every side, the horse lines would be overrun and the cavalry left impotent. Kitchener had little doubt that the superior arms and discipline of his men would in the end win the day but serious bloodshed would be certain and it was possible even to conceive defeat.

But *would* the dervishes attack by night? Was the standard of their discipline high enough, their skill sufficient, to enable them to slip large bodies of men across the open country without alerting the watchful sentries? Was their morale all that was needed to sustain a night attack or would their courage crumble without the flags and the sunshine, the war drums and the moaning of the great ombeya? Slatin's spies reported that the Khalifa intended to march his men round the Kerreri hills during the night and take the allied position in the rear. But was such a march practicable? Was it not more likely that this was a mischievous report, spread to ensure that the Sirdar's army did not pass too tranquil a night? Kitchener did not know; but the danger was real and he decided to do all in his power to mitigate it.

First, he instructed the gun-boats to keep their searchlights on all night, sweeping over the dervish lines and the plains across which an attack would have to come. Fear of snipers made the gun-boats keep to the centre of the river and the lights were not powerful or constant enough to detect all movement, but they could not fail to make an assault more difficult. Then a group of Arabs, brought over from Stuart Wortley's irregular army on the other side of the river, was posted along the ridge of the Jebel Surgham. If they spotted an enemy movement their orders were to move slowly back towards the zariba uttering the characteristic dervish war-cry – a 'rou-rou-rou' continuously repeated and maintained by rapping the lower part of the throat with the hand. The noise was demonstrated to the various British regiments to make sure that, if the time came, there would be no confusion. The junior officers were delighted and spent much of the early evening trying out their new accomplishment; the Warwickshires were particularly pleased with their performance, convinced that they had caught the vibrant, wailing quality of the original.

Finally, Wingate and Slatin took more active steps to deter a night attack. Such villagers as remained in the village of Egeiga were told in strict confidence that the Sirdar was only awaiting the darkness to set his army in march towards the dervishes. This, it was felt, should ensure the news getting to the Khalifa's ears but, in case it did not, two of Slatin's favourite spies were briefed to wander into the enemy lines, posing as deserters, and to tell the same story of an imminent attack. If the Khalifa believed that the infidels were on the way he would surely stand his ground rather than set off to meet them in head-on collision?

Having done all he could, Kitchener tranquilly settled his men down for a good night's rest. He took a calculated risk; it was more important that the soldiers should be able to stretch out and sleep than that enough men should be alert to deal with a sudden and large-scale assault. The flimsy zariba was manned by double sentries at fifty-yard intervals. Every hundred yards a small patrol under an officer was on duty, making occasional expeditions up and down its sector of the front and relieving the sentries at the end of every hour. That was all. Behind them the great bulk of the army was left in peace; every man, as Gatacre insisted, stretched out with his feet pointed towards the enemy, his rifle at his side.

But it was one thing to decree that the army should pass a peaceful night, another to ensure that in fact it did. Exhaustion made it certain that there would be some erratic slumber but a great unease hung over the force, men stirred restlessly as they dozed, one cried out in a dream, another passed the hours in muttered conversation with a neighbour. 'Ah, Tim,' the padre heard one soulful Cameron murmur to another, 'how many thousands there are at home across the sea, a-thinking o' us the nicht!' 'Right, Sandy,' was the unromantic reply, 'and how many millions there are that don't care a damn. Go to sleep, you fule!' The army stirred and rippled like a sea, never wholly still, never silent. 'All our animals were very restless,' noted George Jeffreys, who could not himself have claimed to be entirely calm though he kept up a brave front before his men. 'Camels grunting, mules neighing, while in the desert between the two forces were a lot of pariah dogs and jackals which were terror-stricken and howled most piteously all night . . .' Jeffreys allowed his imagination to run away with him when he read terror into the jackals' cry; if any emotion can legitimately be postulated, the joyful expectation of rich pickings on the morrow would be as likely to be near the mark.

Other people heard other things. Frank Scudamore, of the *Daily News*, was kept awake more dramatically by the cries and shouts of the dervishes – the throbbing of their drums and the raucous moans of their ombeyas. 'There was no doubt about it; they were full of beans.' None of the other listeners who recorded their memories of the scene seem to have been similarly disturbed but Scudamore, after all, was recollecting for a wider audience whose appetite for picturesque detail was no doubt more voracious than the relations and friends of the average soldier. Whether or not the cries, throbs and moans in fact provided so rich a background it is unlikely that any soldier there that night for long forgot that within five miles, perhaps far closer, perhaps even now within a few hundred yards, was an enemy host whose fighting powers had already been amply proved and whose determination to kill every man in the allied army could not be doubted.

It was brilliant moonlight, none of the previous night's heavy rain to dampen morale or cloak the approach of an approaching foe. So much to the good, but such illumination can be an uncertain ally. '. . . Shooting by moonlight is a tricky proceeding,' noted Egerton of the Seaforths, a regiment whose reputation for marksmanship was second to few, 'and eyes down to the sight see very much less than one would expect.' Luckily the same was true for the handful of Arab snipers who had crawled through the darkness to the slopes overlooking the encampment. The use of lights by the Anglo-Egyptian army was strictly forbidden but every so often some impatient soldier, trying to see the time or in search of a suspected scorpion, would break the rule. As often as not this act of folly was followed by the crack of a dervish rifle yet the bullets flew overhead or ploughed harmlessly into the sand. There were no casualties during the night.

Moonlight plays curious tricks on eyes and nerves. To the anxious sentries the great plain in front of them seemed peopled with strange shapes. Surely that rock, or was it a bush, was not exactly where it had been a moment before? Was that not a sudden shadow flitting across the sand? That noise, could it not be the grate of rifle upon rock or the soft pad of feet? One of Jeffreys's sentries came up to him, woke him, 'and told me very coolly that the enemy were advancing in force and would be up in about ten minutes'. Instantly alert, Jeffreys woke his platoon and they manned the zariba. It was a false alarm; only the shadows of clouds scudding in the moonlight. Cursing, the men slouched back to their unsatisfactory couches. Then came fresh disturbance. A camel whose forelegs had been hobbled suddenly elected to resent its posture, rose to its feet and floundered around the camp, knocking over tents and scattering piles of equipment. Startled men leapt to their feet, ready to die bravely in the face of the enemy, then relapsed in mingled relief and fury as the recaptured camel was dragged protesting back to its place.

At 11.30 p.m., it seemed that the night phantoms had at last become reality. Shots were heard from the Jebel Surgham and, moments later, Slatin's scouts came cascading across the sands, roo-roo-rooing for all their worth and panting out that the dervish army was on their heels.

A battalion rushed forward to man the zariba, peering anxiously into the moonlit distance. There was only stillness, the rustle of the breeze, the fleeting shadows. Slowly it dawned on them that this had been another false alarm, the scouts had been panicked by a sniper's shots and had deserted their posts without more ado. 'It says much for the men's discipline that no shot was fired,' commented a'Court. Once more the soldiers returned to rest, this time with the reflection that the last flimsy tripwire between them and the dervishes had been removed.

By midnight half the officers in the army were wide awake, peering into the ghostly vastness from which the enemy would come. 'None of the old hands wished for a night attack,' noted Smith Dorrien, 'although many of the young bloods said, "Let them come on!"' He at least had no doubt on which side his sympathies lay, he had seen too much hand-to-hand fighting at Isandhlwana to wish to have that savage butchery repeated in the Sudan. Gradually the opinion hardened that the dervishes would attack just before first light. Colonel Hatton of the Grenadiers was one of the few officers tough enough in mind and body to sleep through the uproar. It served him little, since soon after midnight he found his brigadier leaning over him to announce that the attack would come at 3.30 a.m. Hatton was not over-impressed by the quality of the staff's intelligence but he gave the necessary orders and returned to sleep again. The last hours before dawn passed in a sort of dazed tranquillity.

Meanwhile a few miles away the other army tossed and muttered in its sleep, peered nervously into the darkness, speculated endlessly about the morrow. Perhaps the dervish soldier feared death less than his British counterpart, perhaps he had less to lose, but no man can be wholly calm on the eve of battle and it is doubtful if the thoughts and prayers of the two armies were so vastly different.

As dusk began to fall the Khalifa called a conference

with all his emirs. As is usual with large meetings the world over, the effort to reach a decision quickly proved too much and the matter was referred to a sub-committee. The Khalifa, Osman Azrak and Sheikh el Din retired into conclave. It is unlikely that they spent much time discussing the possibilities of a night attack. Osman Azrak might have favoured it but the Khalifa knew that only a handful of his men were trained to the level where they could make a success of so ambitious an operation. Anyway, he had been persuaded by Neufeld that the English never did things the same way twice. Having attacked by day at the Atbara they would certainly attack by night at Omdurman. In that case it would be best to wait and destroy them at the end of their march. If dawn came and the infidel had not moved then it would be time enough to think of an attack.

As soon as it was dusk the gun-boats' searchlights began to play on the dervish army. 'What is that strange thing?' asked the Khalifa. 'Sire, they are looking at us!' answered Osman Azrak. Angrily the Khalifa ordered his small white tent to be struck lest it should betray his presence to the enemy. All night as the lights played the dervishes shifted uneasily under the intrusive beam, nagging reminder of the strange powers which the infidels enjoyed, the mysterious and unchivalrous weapons which would be levelled at them on the following day. Shortly after darkness fell, Slatin's spies arrived and were led to the Khalifa. The Turks had dug a deep ditch, they said, in the hope that the dervishes would attack at once, fall into it and be easily destroyed. If there were no such attack then the Turks themselves would march by night. The Khalifa nodded, well satisfied that his judgment had so quickly been proved correct.

And so the two armies waited and watched through the night; each one half-hoping and half-fearing that the other would attack at dawn; each one aware that, even if it did not, the following day must bring the final confrontation.

CHAPTER VII

The Assault on El Egeiga

3.30 a.m. An hour and a half before dawn. The time at which a man's blood traditionally runs thinnest, his resistance to night's phantoms is most frail. A chill wind blew off the desert, the moon had wholly gone, not the faintest tremor of light betrayed the fact that day was round the corner. Cursing and grumbling; spitting and hawking; heads aching, bodies creaking, throats raw from the perpetual wind and sand; the army dragged itself to its feet. It was the stand-to-arms. When the bugles of reveille rang across the desert half an hour later, 20,000 men were already massed behind the zariba, peering out into the darkness in search of the enemy. Every officer had checked the working of his revolver, every Tommy opened the breach of his Lee Metford and tested the action of the magazine. The gun-crews were at their posts, the gun-boats prowled suspiciously along the Nile, dim black shapes against the blacker water. The expeditionary force was ready for whatever was to happen next.

What was to happen next? Not even the Sirdar knew. It depended on the dervishes. If the Khalifa proposed to attack then Kitchener would ask nothing better than to be allowed to welcome him. If he did not, then the army must go in search of him. And what would they find? Would the enemy have stood his ground or might some part of the army at least have slipped back into the city to defend it to the last? Or worse still, might the whole giant army have melted away into the desert? Might Omdurman, after all, not be the final scene of the River War? Was Gordon to remain unavenged for still longer yet?

5.30 a.m. came and there was no sign of the enemy. The Sirdar resolved that he could wait no longer. The army began to form up outside the zariba, shuffling into line, dressing from the right, still peering forward into the grey dawn to the bulk of Jebel Surgham ridge 1200 yards ahead. There was, wrote Bennett, 'a curious look of suppressed excitement in some of the faces . . . the curious gleam which comes from the joy of shedding blood – that mysterious impulse which still holds its own in a man's nature whether he is killing rats with a terrier, rejoicing in a prize fight, playing a salmon, or potting Dervishes'. A disagreeable reflection from a loathsome man, but not for that reason wholly without truth.

Already a contingent of the Egyptian cavalry under Captain Baring had trotted out to the ridge to see what was going on. It was nervous work, stumbling up the hill in near total darkness without knowing whether the land was empty ahead or at any moment they might not find themselves entangled with the dervish army. By the time they had reached the top of the ridge it was light enough to make out something of what lay ahead. A glance was enough to establish the essential fact: the dervish army was still there, that day there was at least to be a battle. Even as they watched the line stirred and began to move forward. There was indeed to be a battle, and soon . . .

For the dervishes the awakening had been no more comfortable. The Khalifa, in particular, had reason to be dismayed for the first news to be given him was that 6000 of his men had deserted during the night. 'The prophecy will be fulfilled, if only five people stay near me,' cried Abdullahi. A proud enough boast, but the sight of their leader on his knees, head bowed to the ground, groaning and calling out to Allah, cannot have provided a cheerful start to the day for the apprehensive dervishes.

One thing at least was evident to Abdullahi. He must

109

attack. There was only one way to rally a demoralised army and that was by advancing in the teeth of the enemy. Besides, he more than half expected that the enemy might prove toothless. Another of the rumours spread by Slatin's spies was that Kitchener had been so appalled by the size of the dervish army that he had decided to retreat while the going was good. The bombardment of the city had been no more than a malevolent farewell. If this was so, then the sooner the Khalifa was on the Sirdar's tail, the better it would be. He would harry the Turks the whole way back to Cairo, not a man would survive to boast to his children about the day he had stood within a few miles of Omdurman.

On the white donkey which he was to ride throughout the battle he moved slowly along the line in front of his men. Stopping here and there he told them of the vision that he had seen during the night. The Prophet and the Mahdi had come to him. They had shown him the souls of the faithful rising to paradise while the legions of hell tore to shreds the spirits of the defeated infidels. Victory would be theirs, paradise would be theirs, their fame would live for ever. They had heard it all before a hundred times but the words were no less potent for the repetition. A wild exaltation caught them up. Death had no sting, defeat no meaning. With a great roar that shook the desert, the multitude lurched forward and was on the move.

The dervish front, stretching between four and five miles across the desert when it began to move, was divided into five main sections. On the extreme left – furthest, that is to say, from the river, under the bright green flag of Ali Wad Helu, were some 5500 men of the Degheim and Kehena tribes, including 800 cavalry. Next came the most numerous contingent, more than 28,000 men from the Jehadia and Mulazemin under the dark green flag of the

Scouts catch first sight of the Dervish force

Khalifa's son, Sheikh el Din. This cohort included some
1200 cavalry but the bulk of the Baggara horsemen were
part of the next division of some 14,000 men under the
Khalifa's brother Yakub and the sacred black flag of the
Mahdi. The Khalifa himself came next, under his own
giant black banner, lettered with texts from the Koran
and the Mahdi's sayings, a sheet two yards square supported on a twenty foot bamboo pole, ornamented at the
top with a silver bowl, spandrel and tassel. Around him
were gathered some 7000 men, mainly from his own
Taiasha tribe. Finally, under the white flags of Osman
Digna and Osman Azrak and the red flag of the Danagla
under Sherif, came a further 8000 men with a handful of
cavalry. Nearly a hundred Emirs and five times as many
sub-emirs marched or rode with their men, each one with
his own personal banner, so that as the great host, 60,000
strong, moved forward, it seemed as if an armada of small
boats had been caught up in a black, irresistible tide and
was being swept willy nilly across the desert.

The army which confronted them was barely half the
size. Kitchener's men were still deployed in the semi-circle
resting on the river which they had adopted the night
before. Nearest Omdurman, and therefore on the part of
the front which theoretically might be expected to bear
the brunt of the attack, was Lyttelton's 2nd Brigade, the

most recent arrivals to the country and the most eager to be blooded, the 1st Battalions of the Northumberland Fusiliers and the Grenadiers, the 2nd Battalions of the Lancashire Fusiliers and of the Rifle Brigade. Wauchope's 1st Brigade, the veterans of the Atbara, resented pride of place thus being given to these tyros. They occupied the next part óf the line; sloping back at an angle of 45° from the Nile. The 1st Battalions of the Warwickshire Regiment, the Lincolns, and the two Highland regiments, the Camerons and the Seaforths, considered themselves an elite body, the most powerful and best disciplined striking force at Kitchener's disposal. Wauchope and his officers had no doubt that, when the time came to storm the city, it would be the 1st Brigade which would lead the assault and burst through the great wall around the Khalifa's palace.

The British Division was roughly 8000 strong. Behind it were grouped twenty-six of the forty-four guns in the Sirdar's army, notably the 32nd Field Battery of the Royal Artillery, the most effective artillery unit in the continent of Africa. They were placed where they were partly because there was a convenient knoll from which they could command the battlefield but more because the full weight of any enemy attack was thought likely to come between the Jebel Surgham and the river and it was only fitting that the cream of the allied artillery should be there to greet them.

At the hinge of the line, between the British and the Egyptian Division, was Major Arkwright with the 2nd (Fortress) company of the Royal Engineers; the team which had contributed so mightily by its work on the desert railway and was now rewarded for its labours by a place on the grandstand for the final act. Then came the first section of the Egyptian Division, Maxwell's 2nd Brigade, with the Sudanese and one Egyptian regiment. Major Townshend, one day to be better known as

Townshend of Kut, commanded the XIIth Sudanese, a regiment whose reputation for bravery under fire was unsurpassed in any part of the Anglo-Egyptian army. Maxwell's brigade was on a line roughly parallel with the river. Sloping back towards the Nile on the north flank, furthest from Omdurman, was Macdonald's★ 1st Brigade, also consisting of three Sudanese and one Egyptian regiment. Hector Macdonald, Old Mac to all his men though less than fifty years in age, was in terms both of personality and of performance one of the most outstanding soldiers in the allied army. Short and enormously broad, 'so sturdily built that you might imagine him to be armour-plated under his clothes,' he looked like what he was, the son of a Ross-shire crofter who, through tenacity and talent, had won his way from the ranks to his present position. But beneath the square, red face, the heavy moustache, the sergeant-major bearing, were eyes of curious gentleness. He was to be the hero of Omdurman, some even said the real victor. Five years later he was accused of sodomy while serving in Ceylon, was brutally rebuffed by King Edward VII and shot himself in a hotel room in Paris. 'What else could you expect from a fellow with his background,' was the attitude of those fellow officers who had fawned on him in public and sniggered behind his back at his table-manners or lack of polished conversation.

Between Macdonald's brigade and the river was the 3rd Brigade under Colonel Lewis. 'Taffy' Lewis was one of the most popular officers in the army, quick, shrewd and vigorous, but the four Egyptian battalions under his command nevertheless had the reputation of being the weakest element under Kitchener's command. If any part of the front crumbled under pressure, it was likely to be here: hence, of course, the brigade's sheltered position at the rear. Finally Collinson's 4th Brigade, with three

★ More often written as MacDonald, but in official documents usually without the second capital.

113

full and one half battalions of Egyptians, was held in reserve with the transport in the centre of the Egeiga encampment.

Outside the zariba the 21st Lancers prowled beside the river and around the Jebel Surgham. Apart from the small detachment under Baring, all the rest of the cavalry, the camel corps and the horse artillery were up in the Kerreri Hills, a mile and a half from the river and slightly behind the main force at Egeiga. Their role was to check any left-flanking movement that the dervishes might seek to throw out through the hills; otherwise it was possible to imagine a sudden attack launched on Lewis's frail Egyptians in the rear while the rest of the army was fully engaged with the main attack in the front. It was taken for granted that, if the dervishes were foolish enough to attack, they would concentrate their greatest weight on the encampment so that Broadwood and the cavalry would only be called upon to deal with light infiltrating forces.

As soon as Baring was satisfied that the forward movement he had seen from the Jebel Surgham was indeed the prelude to all out assault and not some obscure manoeuvre designed to adjust the line, he sent a galloper back to report to Kitchener. In another ten minutes the messenger might have met the army on the move, as it was he arrived in time to check them as they stood expectant on the fringe of the zariba. It did not take Kitchener a moment to revert with relief to the earlier, favourite plan. 'Back we went to our trenches and lay low like ole Brer Rabbit,' wrote Captain Sparks, who would have been extremely offended if he had known that the 3rd Egyptian Brigade with which he served had been put where it was because of doubts about its fighting capabilities. Of course neither he nor any other junior officer was given any indication why tactics were being so rapidly changed but it did not need much acumen to guess that the dervish army was on the way. Fixedly the soldiers stared ahead, waiting for the first sign of enemy activity. Sparks, gazing pessimistically towards his front in the general direction of Cairo, thought it unlikely that anything very dramatic would transpire in his part of the battlefield. He comforted himself with the thought that the battle would certainly be a long one and that there would be time enough for the 3rd Brigade to play its part.

His job done, Baring withdrew from the Jebel Surgham to link up with the rest of the Egyptian cavalry under Broadwood in the Kerreri hills.

His place was taken by a small detachment of the Lancers. 'I was, I think, the first to see the enemy,' wrote Churchill excitedly to Ian Hamilton, 'certainly the first to hear their bullets. Never shall I see such a sight again. At the very least there were 40,000 men – five miles long in lines with great humps and squares at intervals – and I can assure you that when I heard them shouting their war songs from my coign of vantage on the ridge of Heliograph Hill, I and my little patrol felt very lonely. And though I never doubted the issue – I was in great awe.' It was characteristic of Churchill that he took it for granted his role was in some way of unique significance; more characteristic still that he took it upon himself to despatch personally to the Sirdar a report of his observations, obligingly copying the message to his commanding officer; most characteristic of all that he ridiculed his performance when he came to write his history of the campaign – 'as we did not know that the Egyptian squadron had already looked over the ridge, we enjoyed all the excitement without any of the danger.'

Churchill caused some indignation among the Lancer officers by remaining mounted and thus attracting fire from dervish sharpshooters. 'Bullets whistling and splashing on rocks very close,' reported Lt Smyth, who had been sent on ahead with one Lancer to hold his horse while the rest of his patrol sheltered behind the rocks. It was not the additional danger which Smyth resented but the fact that Colonel Martin took alarm and called him back, 'much excited and annoyed and very fussy, saying I was unnecessarily exposing myself.' It was really too bad! 'It was the Correspondent's fault and after all it was only one private and myself, no great loss if we had been hit . . .'

The most striking feature about the dervish advance as reported by Baring and the Lancers was that it seemed in a fair way to miss the Anglo-Egyptian position altogether. Though the units on the extreme right under Osman Digna and Osman Azrak would pass over the Jebel Surgham and therefore come close to Egeiga, the main thrust of the attack was towards the Kerreri hills. Though no record survives to explain the Khalifa's strategy, there can be little doubt that he had totally misunderstood Kitchener's dispositions. For some reason he assumed that the army had abandoned the camp and had been drawn up along the Kerreri range. He was soon to be disillusioned but by that time the unfortunate Broadwood, equipped to do little more than deter small groups of skirmishers, had found himself the target of a massive assault.

The first assurance given to the troops in the encampment that the enemy was really on the move came when a muted buzz, the sound of a swarm of bees at the other end of a large orchard, began to filter across the plain. The noise grew stronger; the beating of drums could be detected, the wail of the ombeya, human voices raised in vast cacophony. Still nothing could be seen. Then a small group of the Lancers appeared over the ridge and trekked sedately towards the zariba. Another group appeared near the summit of the Jebel Surgham, checked and turned back to look in the direction of the city. The Grenadier officers were standing in front of the zariba in which a few holes had been discreetly left by which they could eventually retreat. More than one observer remarked that they looked like a group of race-goers chatting casually as they awaited the appearance of the field at the end of a point-to-point. They would have been pleased by the analogy. But as the noise mounted, the chatter died. 'The strain was intense,' said Bagot. 'I stood watching through a telescope and longing to be able to see what the scouts saw.' A little further from the river a handful of officers from the Seaforths wore the same air of gentlemanly insouciance. An officer of the Lancers galloped up to the zariba, clearly bound towards the Sirdar. 'What's happening?' called out Egerton, who knew him slightly. 'They are coming on beautifully, and are less than two miles off now,' was the reply.

The rustle of anticipation ran down the line. Still nothing could be seen. The Methodist chaplain walked down behind the zariba, shaking hands here and there. 'Four-nine-four,' called out two or three of the men. 'Four-nine-four!' 'Four-nine-four,' repeated Mr Watkins. Hymn Number 494 in *Sacred Songs and Solos* was 'God be with you till we meet again'.

'Just about 6.10 a.m.,' wrote Egerton, 'gazing intently through my glasses, I saw just topping the ridge in front a little white speck – it was the first of the enemy's banners to appear.' Then there was another, and another, and suddenly the whole ridge running down north-west of the Jebel Surgham was covered by a teeming swarm of black dots, coming thicker and faster until it seemed that there could be no more dervishes in Africa. 'It was a sight to be remembered as long as ever life lasts – a pageant that I imagine can never recur.' To Kitchener and his staff the sight meant victory; the enemy had been delivered into their hands. '. . . after our months of labour in the desert,' wrote Rawlinson, 'I felt I could understand Moses's feelings as he looked out from Mount Gizireh.'

There was a curious unreality about the scene. The
dervishes nearest the river had not yet come into view
over the steeper slopes of the Jebel Surgham and it seemed
as if the rest of the Khalifa's army was wholly without
interest in its enemy. Rank upon rank, marching with a
precision that would not have disgraced the Prussian
Guard, they swept on towards the Kerreri hills. By now
it was possible to make out the individual emirs in front
of their men. As the soldiers began to come into focus, so
did the noise they made: what had seemed a wordless,

The Khalifa's army attacking Kitchener's forces at Kerreri

mindless roar could now be heard as a ceaseless chant –
'*La Ilaha illa llah wa Muhammad rasul ullah*', 'There is but
one God and Muhammad is the Messenger of God'.

As Kitchener stood watching, Lt George Gorringe of
the Royal Engineers hurried up to report that all the boats
carrying supplies and ammunition had now been deployed
in their proper places along the bank of the Nile. 'So that
is now in order,' commented the Sirdar. 'We have done
our work. If they cannot win the fight, God help them!'
Already the leading dervishes were beginning to draw

away from the encampment and were dangerously close to Broadwood's tiny force. It was time to act. A word to a staff officer sufficed, a quick message was passed, and at 6.25 a.m. the 32nd Field Battery opened fire at a range of 2700 yards. Almost immediately the Egyptian batteries followed suit and within a few moments the gun-boats too had joined in the barrage. From just behind the line of advancing dervishes a gun responded and sudden plume of reddish sand sprang up 200 yards or so in front of the zariba where General Wauchope was standing. Battle, at last, was truly joined.

For the most part the guns of the expeditionary force were firing shrapnel – 'with splendid effect' as a private in the Seaforths remarked with satisfaction. But to those who knew rather more what to expect, the effect was decidedly disappointing. The aim was excellent but each shell seemed to do no more than send a ripple through the advancing horde. Men must surely be falling and dying beneath the hail of lethal fragments but to the watching British the advance seemed as massive, as irresistible as ever. Quickly, however, the firing was proved to have had one effect at least. As Egerton watched the enemy army it seemed as if a magic wand had suddenly been waved, switching the focus of attention from the distant Kerreri hills to the waiting army at Egeiga. 'The whole of the dervish line suddenly raised a wild battle cry and simultaneously discharged their guns and rifles in one gigantic *feu-de-joie*.' A huge section of the dervish army seemed in an instant to change course, to peel off from the main line of advance and to be bearing down on the encampment. Almost at the same moment another forest of white banners blossomed over the hill between the peak of the Jebel Surgham and the Nile. Swiftly the two floods blended into one, so that the army at Egeiga, which only a few moments before had feared that it might be left on the periphery of the battle, now found itself in the centre of a great crescent of advancing dervishes.

So far virtually all the firing had been confined to the artillery on either side. The British field guns were quick to switch to the new target appearing on their left. As the Lancers, safely back from their reconnaissance, galloped into the zariba, a savage barrage fell on the enemy some 3000 yards behind them. Young Hodgson of the Lincolnshires, itching to fire his first shot in anger, noted the devastation with some disapproval. 'The field guns had the range and slated them most fearfully, so that many sheared off into a hollow on our right.' For a moment it seemed as if the advance had been checked before it had properly begun. But only in one part of the line and only for a few moments did the enemy falter, everywhere else they surged on as if the shells which battered them were no more than flies to be brushed disdainfully aside.

Now another defect in the dervish training became apparent. Though their rifles were antiquated compared with those of the British, even the Egyptians, their riflemen were still numerous and effective enough to be more than troublesome at close range. The nearer they could get to the enemy line before the infantry began to exchange fire, the better it would be for the dervish cause. The Khalifa, however, had been assured that Mahmud had lost the battle of the Atbara because he had held his fire too long. This time he was determined to start in time. His error was quickly evident. It is doubtful if more than one in fifty bullets from the first fusillade reached the allied lines and few of those did any damage. One caused some offence to Major Bagot who had been standing watching the spectacle with detached interest. It was as good as a play: 'black fellows in their white gibbas with coloured patches, line behind line, until one could only see the spear tops of the furthest moving just below the sky-line; the mounted Emirs riding here and there, and

The opening charge of the Dervishes against the British Division

the countless banners, and high above all a large green
standard'. Then a bullet thudded into the ground and the
spectacle suddenly became less absorbing. 'It made me
jump like blazes, and I looked round hurriedly to see if
anyone had noticed. Apparently not, and so I beat a hasty
retreat behind the zariba.'

It was almost time for the infantry to take a hand in
repelling the attack. Lt Pritchard of the Engineers, who
was 'galloper' to the 1st Egyptian Brigade – a sort of
A.D.C. to Colonel Macdonald charged particularly with
communications with the other brigades and the Sirdar –
noted how the traditional posture was taken up: close
order, line formation, front rank kneeling, rear rank
standing. It was only when he saw a re-enactment of the
battle of Waterloo many years later at the Aldershot
tattoo that he realised just how traditional the posture in
fact had been. Indeed, though certainly the weapons had
improved, he could see no indication that the British tac-

The Dervishes advancing to attack

tics had in any way evolved in the intervening seventy years. It was fortunate for Kitchener that the dervishes used tactics which had not varied for seven centuries: almost, indeed, since mankind first had recourse to war.

In fact the Khalifa's tactics were even more foolish than immediately appeared to the British. If he had flung his entire force into one all-out assault on the encampment then it is conceivable, though unlikely, that at some point he might have forced the line. If one of the Egyptian brigades had crumbled then the other troops would have found themselves attacked in front and behind. But the dervishes were not prepared to commit their whole force in an assault on what they still did not believe to be the main allied position. Ali Wad Helu's contingent and the bulk of the troops under Sheikh el Din contained their headlong charge towards the Kerreri hills and the evasive cavalry. Yakub and the Khalifa himself, with over 20,000 men, waited behind the shelter of the Jebel Surgham to see what developed and to decide at leisure where they would be best advised to throw in their weight. The attack on Egeiga was thus made by some 10,000 men from Sheikh el Din's army, temporarily under the command of Osman Azrak, and Osman Digna's 8000 advancing under their white banners between the Jebel Surgham and the river. It was a formidable force, but pitifully inadequate to the task it had been given.

To the men who awaited them, kneeling in the first rank, their enemy seemed neither pitiful nor inadequate. Though clouds of smoke and dust showed where the shells were ploughing into the dervish ranks, the advance continued unchecked. To the officers, watching through their field glasses as the enemy crumbled under the hail of shrapnel or were tossed in broken fragments high into the air by the blast of high explosive shells, the fearful cost was evident; to the men all that was apparent was the solid wall of warriors bearing down on them and the mounting tumult of hysterical hate which rolled across the sand. The angry hum had become a roar, had become a blood-curdling clamour which rose above even the thunder of the artillery. One cry of ear-splitting ferocity out-soared all the rest. 'Take that man alive,' ordered a Grenadier officer. 'We'll need him as first whip for the Khartoum hounds!'

Still the artillery bore the whole burden of repelling the attack. The gunners never slackened in their task; 'it was pound, pound, pound from first to last,' wrote a'Court. But now the nearest dervishes were less than a mile and a quarter from the zariba. Lord Edward Cecil, Kitchener's A.D.C. and son of the prime minister, galloped over to Lyttelton. The 2nd Brigade were to open fire with their Lee Metfords as soon as the brigadier thought it justified. Hurriedly Lt Grenfell got the range from the nearby gunners. Just over 2000 yards. It was a long shot but probably worth it. At 6.35, ten minutes after the field guns had opened fire, the Guards fired their first volley. A few seconds later the Warwicks joined in; then, as the wings of the dervish army began to draw near the zariba, the Highlanders and Lincolns began to play their part. And so the action moved across to embrace Maxwell's 2nd Egyptian brigade, each regimental commander ordering fire as the quality of his weapons and his men's marksmanship made expedient. Last of these to fire was Townshend with the XIIth Egyptians. 'I determined that not a trigger should be pulled until they were 400 yards from us. Many of the men kept looking round to me as much as to say "let us fire now!"' In the end even Townshend's cool resolution faltered and the XIIth Egyptians were allowed to open fire when the dervishes were still a generous 600 yards away. At 6.45 a.m. Lewis's 3rd Egyptian brigade entered the fray and now the whole centre of the line was on fire. Only at the extremities where a frustrated Rifle Brigade and Lancashire Fusiliers and a slightly less belligerent 7th and 15th Egyptian regiments observed the battle from their perches beside the Nile was there any tranquillity to be found.

The bulk of the attacking force was still no more than a menacing blur in the distance but the occasional individual was beginning to become distinct. Captain Ray of the Northumberland Fusiliers was amazed to see 'an emir on a coal black horse cantering straight towards the zariba. He was hundreds of yards in front of the rest, and made a striking picture (as well as target), his white clothing showing up in strong relief against his black charger. As he came on, never altering his speed either to go faster or slower, with an absolute contempt of death, all who saw him were moved to admiration. Suddenly, when quite close to the zariba, he disappeared and was seen no more'. In the end it was established that, after the front line of three regiments had blazed away at him fruitlessly, a sergeant of the Cameron Highlanders had bowled him over.

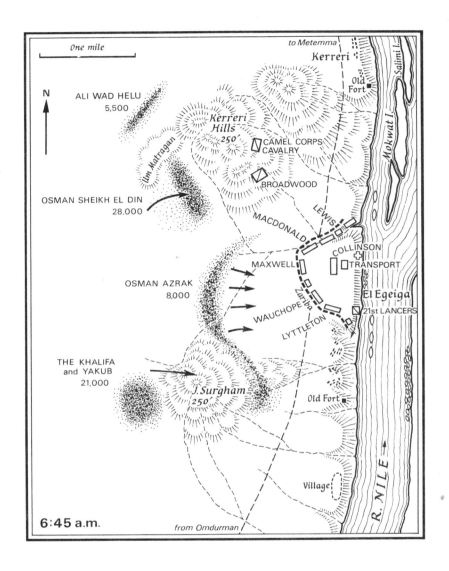

One mile

N

ALI WAD HELU
5,500

Um Matragan

Kerreri Hills
250'

CAMEL CORPS
CAVALRY

BROADWOOD

OSMAN SHEIKH EL DIN
28,000

MACDONALD

LEWIS

COLLINSON

MAXWELL

Zariba

TRANSPORT

OSMAN AZRAK
8,000

El Egeiga

WAUCHOPE

21st LANCERS

LYTTLETON

THE KHALIFA
and YAKUB
21,000

J. Surgham
250'

Old Fort

to Metemma
Kerreri

Old Fort

Salimi I.

Mokwat I.

R. NILE

Village

6:45 a.m.

from Omdurman

Most battles since the invention of gunpowder have been
in part at least shrouded in a pall of smoke. On September
2, 1898, there was a curious clarity. The prevailing wind,
perhaps, took much of the smoke away; the Lee Metfords
using cordite anyway produced little, the Egyptian infantry did not fire their antiquated Martini-Henrys fast

126

enough to yield the thick white cloud which they could produce in more experienced hands. The whole battle-field lay exposed to Kitchener and his staff as they took up their position behind the Camerons: the field guns and howitzers blasting perpetual defiance; the thin khaki line of the infantry, the mass of the dervishes, racked by bullet and shrapnel yet rolling ever closer. 'The Sirdar sat stolidly upon his horse,' noted one junior staff-officer, 'and at this period of the day no expression upon his face gave evidence of any emotion. The only evidence of what he must really have felt was in the many short questions which he shot incessantly at the various members of his staff.'

One order he quickly gave. It seemed absurd to keep the Rifle Brigade and Lancashire Fusiliers sitting futilely on a flank without an enemy within 3000 yards of them and so they were ordered to double down the line and take up a position in support forty yards behind the Highland regiments. By this time the dervishes were near enough to ensure that their rifle fire was reasonably effective. Private Dillon of B Company, Northumberland Fusiliers, was the first man in the army to be wounded, but the regiments running behind the line quickly found themselves in a painfully vulnerable position. It was a disagreeable business to expose oneself in this way and the Rifle Brigade, who anyway prided themselves that they could march as fast as the ordinary infantry regiment could double, covered the ground with exceptional speed even by their own high standards. The going was rough all the same. 'One man in my company about six inches from me was hit on the head with a bullet,' wrote a Green Jacket major, 'another in the company ahead of me was badly wounded in the groin . . . we all had narrow shaves.'

Nor were their troubles over when they reached their new position. They found themselves perched on top of a small rise directly behind the Seaforths with a grandstand

Kitchener directing the battle

view of the whole battlefield. It is in the nature of a grandstand that it can as easily be seen as seen from, and the Rifle Brigade's vantage point was no exception. They were quickly exposed to the enemy fire and would happily have sacrificed their view of the fighting for a little protection from the bullets. From just after 7 a.m. until 8.20 a.m. they remained conspicuous, squatting disconsolately on the ground and waiting to see who would be the next victim. 'It was not particularly pleasant sitting down to be fired at with no means of retaliation,' commented the same officer. His men would have shared his view, though probably not expressed themselves with such dulcet resignation.

The Rifle Brigade were by no means the only sufferers. Rawlinson, galloping back to the Sirdar with news about the reserves of ammunition, 'heard a crack, and Arrow, my best charger and very good friend, dropped on his knees. Blood was pouring from his nose to such an extent as to ruin my coat and breeches'. Rawlinson had been brought down behind the Warwicks. Almost at the same moment Captain Caldecott, famed as the strongest man and best athlete in the army, fell unconscious as a falling ball took him in the temple and came out through the jugular vein. He lay thus for an hour, came to, pleaded for water, drank and died. Others near him were luckier. Maclachan of the Camerons suddenly felt his side drenched, as he supposed, with blood. Looking down he saw that it was his water bottle which was the victim. Another bullet immediately passed through his ammunition pouch, cutting eight cartridges in half between the lead and the cordite without exploding a single one. A private in the Lincolnshires got a bullet in his haversack which lodged in his red-bound prayer book neatly inscribed 'Nile Expedition, 1898'. 'If he had been an R.C. it would have been a miracle,' remarked Hodgson drily.

But incidents of this kind, whether fatal or near misses, were very much the exception. By 7.30 a.m., when the dervish onslaught first wavered, there were no more than fifty or sixty casualties in the whole expeditionary force. Such losses were miniscule compared with the carnage among the attackers. For more than an hour the advancing dervishes had been blasted by more than 10,000 rifles, as well as the full weight of the allied artillery, including several of the gun-boats. The Sirdar's men had fired until the rifles grew too hot to hold and had to be exchanged for others taken from the troops in support, until the Maxims bucked and jumped like kicking horses while the water in their barrels boiled furiously. The target was one which even the most inexpert could hardly miss. And yet the dervishes had come on, rank upon rank crumpling into twitching heaps in the face of the murderous fire, their successors trampling over their bodies to carry the standards a few painful yards closer to the infidels before they too joined their comrades in paradise. First into battle and first to fall were always the Emirs, rallying their men with the last breath in their bodies, some of them dressed in chain-mail and carrying swords which had been captured from the Christians 600 years before in the Crusades. Today their arms were to pass back into infidel hands in

Copyright.

1. Mahdi's Tomb.	5. Dervish Encampment.	9. Pennon of Head Quarters.
2. Khartum.	6. British Hospital.	10. 2nd Rifle Brigade.
3. Jebel Surgham.	7. Camel Corps.	11. Lancashire Fusiliers.
4. Um Nutragar.	8. Sirdar and Staff.	12. Northumb. Fusiliers.

OMDURMAN—THE

SEPTE

(IN ORDER THAT THE POSITIONS OF THE DIFFERENT REGIMENT

STORY OF THE BATTLE TOLD IN HEADLINES :—Reconquest of the Soudan—Sir Herbert Kitchener's brilliant Victory—Gordon's murderers punis
The highest gift of Generalship—Splendid courage and discipline of British, Soudanese and Egyptian Troops—"A Second Balaclava

TTLE—6.30 a.m.

8.

(UISHED, THE HOME UNIFORMS HAVE BEEN RETAINED.)

completely annihilated—The Sacred City of the Dervishes captured—A horrid system of Government overthrown—Mahdism fallen for ever—

savage daring and heroism—Mowed down by modern weapons of war. THE WAY CLEARED FOR CIVILIZATION.

13. Grenadiers.
14. Lancers.
15. Warwicks.
16. Cameron Highlanders.

17. Seaforth Highlanders.
18. Lincolns.
19. Soudanese & Egyptians.
20. 3 Batteries—Maxims.

21. Maxims.
22. Bearers changing hot rifles.
23. Gunboats.

G. W. BACON & CO., Ltd., LO

the battle which proved for ever that ancient faith alone was powerless when pitted against the full weight of the new technology.

'The valour of those poor half-starved dervishes in their patched jibbahs would have graced Thermopylae.' So wrote Townshend, himself no bad judge of heroism. He spoke for the whole army. The dervishes gained 20,000 admirers that day – little though the thought would have consoled them as they painfully realised that they faced defeat. 'What they lacked in arms they assuredly made up in bravery,' recorded Bagot, himself by now a casualty. 'The whole of the time fighting was going on I never saw a dervish run off the field . . . their retirement was a haughty stalk of offended dignity.' Not many were left to retire.

In front of the British division, where the firing was more intense and accurate, hardly a man got within 800 yards of the zariba. Against the Sudanese and Egyptians the dervishes did better. At 500 yards, already battered but still a coherent fighting force, they broke into a frantic run. The smoke from the Martini rifles gave partial cover so that for a moment their onward rush was obscured. No one could tell what progress was being made; it seemed as if they might even reach the line and come to grips with their hated adversary. Lt Blakeney, another of Kitchener's engineer officers who had done good work on the railway and had been rewarded with a job as galloper, was standing where the action was hottest, just behind the 2nd Brigade. Apprehensively he watched while 'Egyptian subalterns urged their men to keep their muzzles down, and senior officers on horseback stared into the smoke and waited for it to lift'. With precision and discipline which would have been inconceivable a few years before the Sudanese fired volley after volley into the fog of dust and smoke. When at last it dispersed 'only three dervishes – the centre one with a standard – remained to rush to certain death'.

Hodgson, watching through field glasses, takes up the tale. 'I never could have imagined anything so cool and brave as those men were, especially one, the last but one to fall. He had been wounded in his arm and limped, yet his ambition was to get the flag, and he got it and carried it some fifty yards at a sort of slow trot, when he was shot, and as he fell his companion took it and came on a few yards only, when he fell, with the flag.' An old man, bearded, clutching his white banner as if it was his passport to paradise, folded his arms across his face; his limbs loosened and he sprawled ungainly to the earth. He was still more than 200 yards from his objective. 'That was a *man*,' said a ranker from the Warwicks. 'These black chaps know how to fight and how to die.' From behind him Blakeney heard a familiar voice sum up the situation in a rather different vein. 'Cease fire, please! Cease fire! Cease fire,' called the Sirdar. 'What a dreadful waste of ammunition.'

But it was not yet all over. A group of dervish riflemen, perhaps thirty or forty in all, had gone to ground behind a small ridge a few hundred yards in front of the Camerons. There they stuck, and quickly showed how different the course of the battle might have been if the Khalifa had used more subtle tactics. Now the Highlanders had cause to regret that they had not troubled to dig a trench and were dependent for their protection on a flimsy thorn zariba. John Ewart of the Camerons ducked automatically as a bullet zipped overhead, then stood upright with self-conscious bravado. 'Bullets began to hum past in an unpleasant fashion and for some minutes the call of "stretcher" was too painfully frequent.' In less than a quarter of an hour twenty-five Camerons and twelve Seaforth Highlanders had been killed or severely wounded. It was too hot to last. Stewart's Egyptian battery were rushed into the line to help dislodge the hidden enemy and began to lob their shells over the crest of the ridge into the hollow from which the firing seemed to come. 'Bouquets of shrapnel and constant volleys from the Camerons and the Seaforths soon effected our purpose,' concluded Ewart triumphantly, 'and we had the satisfaction of seeing our friends in front rise up and retire, amidst a perfect hail of bullets.'

The importance of the artillery's role in repelling the attack cannot be over-estimated. Keppel, who watched the dervish advance from the vantage point of a gunboat tower, said bluntly that the gunners won the day, by the time they had finished with the attackers only the broken remnants were left for the infantry to shoot down. Nor were the foot-soldiers themselves any more sparing in their praise. 'Our chance of a good show was entirely spoilt by the Artillery,' wrote Captain Ray in mild resentment, 'but really they shot so splendidly that one ought not to grumble that they killed them all before they came properly under our fire.'

'They came very fast, and they came very straight, and then presently they came no further.' Steevens's laconic description of this first phase of the battle is adequate enough as a summary. Almost 18,000 of the Khalifa's best troops had shattered themselves against the Anglo-Egyptian line, 2,000 at least were stretched dead upon the field, twice as many lay where they had fallen, awaiting death, or had crawled painfully away with shattered limbs and bleeding wounds. As a fighting force Osman Digna's famed white flags had ceased to exist. The Sirdar's army was content – they were, after all, so patently the victors – yet not proud of their achievement nor eager to do as much again. It had been a massacre, not a battle, and not much glory had been won by those who ran the slaughterhouse. 'Well, thank God that job's over,' said Egerton of the Seaforths, and he spoke for every soldier in the army.

CHAPTER VIII

'A Close Shave for the Camel Corps'

MEANWHILE, in another part of the field, things almost turned out very differently. On the Kerreri hills Colonel Broadwood was waiting with nine squadrons of Egyptian cavalry massed in the centre of the ridge, the camel corps to his right and the horse artillery spread out along the crest. It was a powerful group, more than adequate for the minor role which had been assigned to it but neither intended nor equipped to resist a major assault. Yet it was precisely with this that Broadwood was now threatened. Though a large section of the dervish centre had swung away to attack the encampment at Egeiga, Ali Wad Helu's 5500 men and at least 15,000 infantry from the Sheikh el Din's massive army careered on towards Kerreri. An officer of the Egyptian cavalry standing near Broadwood looked down in some astonishment at the unexpected sight.

'Yesterday all was silence and some faint dots in the far distance alone indicated the existence of any dervishes. Now, almost at our feet, a very sea of dervishes extended across the plain, and advanced in great uneven masses like waves upon a beach. Here and there a mass of men, meeting some stony hill, would pass round it, crowding in and partly overrunning its sides much as a wave surges round a reef of rocks, and all the while a ceaseless roar arose of many voices shouting a monotonous war-cry mingled with the beating of tom-toms and the braying of war horns.'

But there was no time to stand and stare. A substantial section of the advancing dervishes – in fact the left wing under the green standard of Ali Wad Helu – had swung round to the north of the Kerreri hills and halted, temporarily at least, but the main force was by now at the foot of the range and already beginning to scramble up towards the waiting cavalry. A galloper was soon with the Sirdar, reporting this unexpected news. Kitchener hurriedly sent an order to Broadwood that he should disengage to the south and take shelter within the zariba.

Broadwood, however, had already reached a different conclusion. If he did as he was told and fell back on the encampment at Egeiga, he would have the full force of Sheikh el Din on his tail. The brunt of the attack would be bound to fall on Lewis's Egyptian brigade, notoriously the weakest section of the line; and the anyway nervous defenders would find their task made doubly difficult by the need to let the cavalry scramble home before they could open fire on the dervish line. The result might have been disastrous for the Egyptian brigade and extremely inconvenient, to say the least, for the whole army. Before Kitchener's aide de camp could reach him, therefore, Broadwood had already given orders for a fighting withdrawal towards the north, away from Egeiga, in the hope that a large number of the dervishes would follow and be drawn away from the danger area. The Marquis of Tullibardine, Kitchener's aristocratic emissary, was sent scurrying back to the Sirdar with the news that the movement had already started and that it was now too late to fall back directly on Egeiga.

Captain Green-Wilkinson of the Rifle Brigade had been temporarily attached to the Camel Corps. 'At 5.40 a.m., when the first shot was fired, we had our Maxims and four companies of blacks in line on the ridge, and four companies of Egyptians in reserve and guarding our camels. Fifteen thousand dervishes detached themselves from the main body and advanced against us at a run, chanting war cries. Conspicuous among the many banners was a huge light green flag by which their line was apparently guided and dressed. We opened fire, but failed to check the advance.' By the time the order to retire was given the nearest dervishes were within 300 yards and every feature of their hate-contorted faces seemed horrifyingly clear to the little group of defenders. They scrambled pell-mell back towards their camels; by the time they reached them the dervish advance guard was already swarming over the position which they had so recently occupied.

Ideally Broadwood would have liked to have kept the Camel Corps with the rest of the cavalry in their move to the north, but this would have involved their retreating right across the face of the enemy advance. Regretfully he ordered them to disengage and fall back on the zariba as best they could. It was an order more easily given than obeyed. On the move, deep in the desert, the Camel Corps was a noble spectacle; not even the canvas poke bonnets which the animals wore to protect them against sunstroke could reduce their romantic appeal. They were also remarkably effective; covering great distances across the sands at a speed which left the rest of the army trailing in their wake. But on the rocky slopes of the Kerreri hills, with razor sharp stones and thorns to slash the tender soles of their feet and treacherous holes to snap the legs of the unwary, the camels floundered helplessly. Over the rough ground the heavily laden animals could hardly manage six miles an hour, the pace of the dervish advance was near to eight.

The rearguard under Captain Hopkinson swung round to cover the retreat. It was met by a blast of fire from the advancing dervishes. 'There was a thud, like a fist sinking into flesh, and I felt my beast lurch under me. It sank down on its knees and twisted round its neck, so that its huge brown eyes flecked with a septic yellow seemed to be staring reproachfully at me. Its mouth was open in a grimace of pain and a thick trickle of black blood oozed from the corner and smeared the brown of its hide. It uttered a despairing "grunk", half groan, half wail, and keeled slowly over till it lay twitching feebly on its side.' The camel was not the only one to die; a native officer and several of the men were killed and Hopkinson himself severely wounded. Tullibardine now galloped back with orders that the Camel Corps should immediately fall back on the zariba. With pardonable irritation Hopkinson pointed out that that was what they were trying to do. It seemed increasingly unlikely, however, that they would be able to perform the Sirdar's bidding.

The Horse Artillery had meanwhile delayed its departure dangerously long in an attempt to cover the Camel Corps's retreat. By the time the last guns began to move the dervishes were almost on them. One of the 'wheelers' of the horse battery was shot. Frantically the men swarmed round it trying to cut the traces, but it was impossible to get the dead horse free in time. Then another gun crew – a 7-pounder Krupps – galloped up to see in what way they could help. They did no more than compound the confusion. A wheel caught in the entangled wreckage on the ground, the 7-pounder lurched and capsized, and by now the dervishes were within a hundred yards. The guns would have to be abandoned. Pell mell, two on a horse or clinging on to the stirrup of a friend, the crews fled from the scene. Triumphantly the advancing enemy swarmed over the carcases of the two guns and began, rather ineptly, to try to get them working and on the move.

The cavalry hung around on the fringes, ready to come to the rescue if all else failed. Douglas Haig was in charge of the leading squadrons whose job it was to keep in contact with the dervishes, check their advance so far as was possible and never give the enemy a moment of peace in which they could look around them and decide what would be their most profitable target. He did his duty nobly. Rawlinson, arriving with fresh instructions from the Sirdar, noticed that 'his confident bearing seemed to have inspired his fellaheen, who were watching the dervish advance quite calmly'. The nagging presence of these little bands; impertinently challenging the vast horde which confronted them; dismounting, firing, remounting, repeating the process again and again always within two or three hundred yards of the dervish swords and rifles; drew the bulk of Sheikh el Din's army towards the north, away from the stricken Camel Corps.

But the corps was still in serious trouble and more than enough dervishes were on their tails to ensure that they would be slaughtered if the enemy caught up with them. Bumping and slithering, every so often one of their number crashing helplessly to the ground, they tumbled down the flank of the Kerreri hills on to the open plain which led towards the Nile and the shelter of the zariba. But the going was still rough and there was more than 2000 yards between them and safety. The dervishes were closing at every moment and it did not need a mathematician to calculate that the gap between hunter and prey would vanish altogether before sanctuary was gained. The bulk of the Egyptian cavalry under Broadwood had now debouched from the main hills and were on the slopes of the lesser range which rose behind them to the north. The leading units of the dervish force were unpleasantly close and the cavalry should already have resumed their retreat, but instead they hovered hesitantly, peering into the dust and smoke which obscured the fighting. To charge across such broken ground into the thick of the dervishes would have been hideously expensive, perhaps even suicidal, but Broadwood would have done it rather than leave his comrades of the Camel Corps to be overrun and massacred.

He was saved from having to make so disagreeable a

decision. Lt Roberts had been sent by the Sirdar to summon gun-boats to the rescue. He signalled to Monkey Gordon in the *Melik* who at once hurried downstream. By the time Gordon arrived the Camel Corps was only some three quarters of a mile from the river but was being harried from the rear and, still more dangerously, were being cut off from the zariba by a fresh wave of dervishes pouring down from the hills to the right of their line of retreat. These were already being shelled from the zariba but the range was long and the fire ineffective. The moment Gordon joined in, the situation was transformed. The *Melik* carried two Nordenfeldt guns, one quick-firing 12-pounder, one howitzer and two Maxims. Supported by another gun-boat of similar class it now began to fire everything it had at the advancing enemy. The effect was literally devastating. The packed masses of the enemy were shattered by the fire which burst upon them, leaving great pools of dead and writhing wounded where only an instant before there had been triumphant warriors scenting victory. Those in front fell, those behind wavered, the advance was checked.

The *Abu Klea* now began to take a hand. 'Estimating the range at about one mile,' wrote its commander, Newcombe, 'I ordered my gunners to open fire with the Krupp; but they were so excited, and so inaccurate in elevation and direction, that after several shots I laid the gun myself. The direction was then correct, but I found that the target was out of range.' To the dervishes, however, the apparition of yet another gun-boat intent on their destruction was more than they could endure. The Camel Corps had by this time reached a point where they could no longer be cut off from Egeiga and safety. They had suffered nearly fifty casualties but they were still a coherent fighting force, retreating under stress but in good order. The attack had failed. Frustrated and enraged, the dervishes drew off.

The gunboat 'Melik' saves the Camel Corps from annihilation

Now was the moment when they should have regrouped and prepared to get back into the main battle against the encampment. Instead they cast around for some other adversary against whom they could launch themselves. They found it in Broadwood's cavalry which, now the Camel Corps was out of danger, was resuming its leisurely retreat towards the north. 'The Horse Artillery battery,' noted Newcombe approvingly, 'in perfect order, stopped and fired, then retired, then stopped and fired again.' The cavalry allowed the leading dervishes to get within range, held them for a few moments with accurate volleys, then mounted and fell back to the next position. When a group of Sheikh el Din's cavalry joined in the pursuit, a brisk charge by a squadron under Major Mahon put them to flight. It was a wholly successful manoeuvre. Though the emirs tried frantically to control their men, the best part of 10,000 dervishes had been drawn two miles away from the scene of real action, the Egyptian section of the

141

zariba had been left unassailed and Sheikh el Din's contingent was going to find itself disastrously out of place at a later stage of the battle.

By shortly after half past eight the first phase of the battle was concluded. Broadwood, looping back along the banks of the Nile down a path cleared for him by the gunboats, was on the point of re-entering the zariba. Within the encampment the Camel Corps was licking its wounds and preparing for the renewal of fighting. Around the perimeter firing had almost spluttered out; only the occasional rifle shot rang out as the last dervishes were winkled out of their positions. It was time for the Sirdar to take stock. The left wing of the dervish advance had swept past the encampment and was lost somewhere in the Kerreri hills. The right and centre, so far as he knew, had dashed itself to destruction against the zariba. Though certain apologists have claimed that he was in fact much better informed than appeared from his actions, there is no reason to believe he suspected the existence of an uncommitted force lurking behind the Jebel Surgham. Certainly he did not for an instant conceive that any such body could be more than 20,000 strong. Nor did he know that Ali Wad Helu's 5500 men had swung to the left of the cavalry's position in the Kerreri hills and had been in no way involved in the subsequent fighting.

Stuart-Wortley, still with the Friendlies on the other side of the river, was standing on the bank of the Nile, looking toward Egeiga where the firing had now died down, and wondering how the battle had gone. He saw a dervish swimming towards him across the river. 'Are you the General?' called the man. Stuart-Wortley replied that the general was on the other side. 'Then, in the name of Allah, tell him that this attack was delivered only by the sweepings of Omdurman, and that the Khalifa is waiting for him behind the Jebel Surgham with the flower of his army and will eat him up if he moves.' Stuart-Wortley tried to send a message across the river by heliograph but it was too late; the army was already on the move and nobody had time to waste keeping in touch with outlying detachments.

Even if Kitchener had received the message it is doubtful if he would have altered his plans to any real extent. For him the all-important consideration was that a large number of dervishes had survived the attack on the encampment. Many of these were unwounded and fully capable of carrying on the fight. At the moment they were falling back across the desert to Omdurman. If they were given a chance to re-enter the city they would dig themselves in and all the good which had flowed from the Khalifa's original mistake would be undone. It was essential that they should be harried and either captured or driven far off into the desert while the Sirdar's army occupied Omdurman and put an end for ever to the Mahdist empire. If Kitchener had known of the forces still pitted against him he would have disposed his forces differently but the timing and direction of the advance would have been very much the same. There was, indeed, nothing else for him to do.

CHAPTER IX

The Charge of the 21st Lancers

BEFORE embarking on an advance into country hidden from view behind a hill, it was an elementary precaution to send ahead the cavalry to look over the top and report on any possible hazards. Broadwood and his Egyptians were still well away to the north; here, at last, was a role for the 21st Lancers. Colonel Martin was instructed to advance over the ridge between the Jebel Surgham and the Nile and to reconnoitre the ground beyond. 'Annoy them as far as possible on their flank,' read the Sirdar's terse instruction, 'and head them off if possible from Omdurman.' It was straightforward enough, and though the Sirdar may have had slight qualms about Colonel Martin's lack of experience under these conditions, he had no doubt that the Lancers were fully competent to perform their task.

Nor did the Lancers. In his letters at the time – though not, of course, in his published history of the campaign – Winston Churchill made no secret of the dislike and contempt he felt for his fellow-officers. His feelings were heartily reciprocated, and not without good reason, but there is no doubt that he had some grounds for his sentiments of superiority. A glance at their regimental photographs suggests the reason why. A group of dummies, draped in attitudes of self-conscious arrogance, stare with glazed complacency across the years towards us. Their full, well-nourished features, their heavy moustaches, their bovine listlessness, tell of a *herrenvolk* who worshipped

Officers and attached officers of the 21st Lancers, 1898

sport and fashion and viewed with distaste the pleasures of the mind. They seem as irrelevant to the problems of modern life, to the problems of life at all, as the duck-billed platypus or the coelacanth. This description – like almost every group-photograph of the period – is, of course, a caricature: all of these officers were brave, some of them were intelligent and open-minded. Nevertheless, a cavalry regiment at the end of the nineteenth century was not a repository of original thinking, nor was their officers' mess a place in which tradition was habitually put in question. Faced with an emergency they would react with courage, certainly, but not with imagination or any degree of enterprise.

To make matters worse, the 21st Lancers were spoiling for a fight. They were acutely conscious of the fact that they were as yet unfledged and were determined to emerge from the battle with at least a modicum of glory. So far, they felt indignantly, Broadwood's Egyptian cavalry had been given an unfair share of the action. Now at last it was their turn. From this attitude grew the most dramatic single action of the battle; an incident fatuous in its con-

145

ception and futile in its consequences but which appealed to the public as an epic to be remembered when all the dreary business of winning a war had been long forgotten. The Charge of the 21st Lancers at Omdurman has been inscribed in the pantheon of romantic recollections in letters only a little smaller than the charge of its sister regiment, the 17th Lancers, in the Light Brigade at Balaclava. The two events rival each other, not only in their intrinsic lunacy but also in the redeeming heroism of the protagonists.

The charge at Omdurman also enjoyed an unusual advantage. Among the participants was a chronicler capable of transmuting even the dreariest incident to flamboyant glory and of weaving pure poetry out of the genuine drama of the charge. Certainly the exploit of the Lancers would never have gained the renown it has but for the participation of Lt Churchill and the superb account which he left of it. It would be impossible – even worse, it would be insolent folly – to stray too far from the pattern of his narrative, even though it has subsequently been enriched by other accounts and by his own private letters.

At about 8.45 a.m., when the firing had died away and the army was standing around in brief relaxation awaiting further orders, General Gatacre, with a group of his staff officers, came galloping along the line towards the Lancers. A rapid conference, a gesture, and the regiment was on its way – 'a great square block of ungainly brown figures and little horses, hung all over with water-bottles, saddle-bags, picketing-gear, tins of bully-beef, all jolting and jangling together; the polish of peace gone: soldiers without glitter; horsemen without grace; but still a regiment of light cavalry in active operation against the enemy'. Behind them the infantry watched them clatter away into the distance, two patrols pushing ahead to inspect the ridge. From there they could see across the plateau to Omdurman; but not, of course, round the corner to

146

where Yakub's army was sheltering behind the mass of the Jebel Surgham.

The ground across which they trotted was no place for a squeamish man. 'Horrible sight of dead and dying,' commented Lt Smyth in the staccato phrases which were his literary trademark, 'wounded horses and men trying to get away. Men on all fours, creeping, finally giving up and lying down to die. Horses neighing and galloping about aimlessly. A regular inferno . . .'

Suddenly a heliograph began to stutter out its message from that distant hill. A signaller from the Seaforths' took down what was said and at once ran with it to Captain Egerton. 'About 400 enemy on hill to our front where we saw them yesterday,' ran the message. 'What are your orders?' Egerton hastened to the Sirdar who was on the right centre of the zariba peering intently up at the Kerreri hills where Broadwood and the cavalry had disappeared from view. He glanced at the scrap of paper. 'Wait!' he ordered tersely. Half a minute passed; then: 'Tell him to worry them on their flank and head them off from Omdurman.' With relief the Lancers resumed their advance, two patrols again pushing ahead to give advance information on the perils in their path.

Trumpeter Steele, at seventeen the youngest man with the regiment, one of the youngest indeed in the whole British force, was with the group which pushed on towards Omdurman under the adjutant, Lt Pirie. They picked their way between groups of dervishes, straggling back towards the city, and several times were fired on by tribesmen whose pugnacity had not been blotted out by their recent tribulations. Then, straight ahead of them and protecting the route which most of the fugitives were following, Steele saw 'a group of about 700 fuzzy-wuzzies' drawn up and confronting the English horsemen with the apparent intention of checking their further advance. Clearly Pirie's little band could venture no further; hurriedly they turned and galloped back to the main body to report what they had seen.

For Colonel Martin the situation was admirably clear. So long as the enemy force remained in its present position, he would be hampered in his designated task of heading off the defeated dervishes who were flocking back to Omdurman; equally he would be prevented from completing his reconnaissance and seeing what enemy force, if any, might be sheltering in the lee of the Jebel Surgham. Seven hundred dervishes standing exposed on open ground could hardly be expected to withstand the charge of 400 British cavalry, let alone 400 Lancers. They would be cut to pieces, dispersed in shattered fragments, thus providing an agreeable blooding for the regiment and an honourable gloss to the battle honour which would shortly be theirs. The order was at once given to continue the advance.

Trumpeter Steele had been pretty accurate in his estimate though Pirie made the total nearer to 1000. The force was of Hadendoa tribesmen, under Osman Digna's flag, who had been stationed there to protect the Khalifa's lines of communication with Omdurman. What Martin could not know, however, was that, as soon as Osman Digna heard that the cavalry had left the zariba and were advancing towards his outpost, he ordered reinforcements to be sent. Two thousand men from Yakub's army of the black flag, under the command of the Emir Ibrahim Khalil hastened to the scene and arrived shortly after Pirie had returned to his regiment. A deep khor ran directly behind the position now occupied by the Hadendoa detachment; in it the reinforcements concealed themselves, as well as over half the original party. When Colonel Martin led his regiment on to the ground all he saw was a group of two or three hundred blue-clad tribesmen impudently defying him. It was one of the oldest and favourite tricks in the Arab repertoire; Broadwood would have been immediately suspicious, Martin had no such

148

qualms. His only regret was that Pirie had over-estimated the task; there were hardly enough enemy to give the Lancers' coming victory any real distinction.

He did, however, take the precaution of inspecting the dervish position from the other flank. This involved moving the regiment at a trot across the enemy front a mere 300 yards away. The challenge was eagerly accepted, the dervish soldiers dropped on to their knees and opened fire. Their first volley brought several horses and riders crashing to the ground. 'My right-hand man dropped, his horse shot under him,' recorded Lt Sykes. 'Bullets seem to be whistling and splashing all around.' There were only two courses open, wrote Churchill to Ian Hamilton, 'Left wheel into Line and gallop off – coming back for the wounded – a bad business; and Right wheel into Line and charge. I think everybody made his own decision. At any rate while the trumpet was still jerking we were all at the gallop towards them. . . . The only order given was Right Wheel into Line. Gallop and Charge were understood.'

Two hundred and fifty yards and the fire came fast and furious. 'Their bullets struck the hard gravel into the air, and the troopers, to shield their faces from the stinging dust, bowed their helmets forward, like the Cuirassiers at Waterloo.' A hundred and fifty yards, and if there was any shooting still going on it was lost in the thunder of the hooves and the hectic exhilaration of the moment. 'It was like going up the straight in the Grand Military,' said one Lancer officer, 'and the line of dervishes seemed as harmless as any winning post.' A hundred yards and suddenly, devastatingly, the trap was sprung. It was as if the ground opened before their startled eyes; what an instant before had seemed level plain was now revealed as a deep ditch, densely packed with white robed men, twelve deep and stretching almost from one end of the cavalry front to the other.

Even if they had wanted to, the Lancers could hardly

The Charge of the 21st Lancers at the battle of Omdurman
Painting by R. Caton Woodville

have checked their charge in time. No such thought, of course, entered their heads; instead they spurred on their horses in a desperate effort to gather the momentum which would carry them through to the other side. The luckless dervishes who had acted as bait were bowled backwards down the bank of the khor on top of their compatriots and with a crash like a great wave surging over a breakwater the Lancers, literally, fell upon their enemies. 'Slap! It was just like that!' said one captain; bringing his fist hard into his open palm as he tried to convey the impression to a friend in the infantry.

A few seconds of stupefaction followed. Some nineteen stone of solid matter hurling down at twenty miles per hour is not a missile to be ignored and the impact shattered the dervish masses like an exploding bomb. It took an instant for men to pick themselves up, recover their senses, gather up their weapons. But then they fought ferociously. They attacked man and horse with everything that came to hand, discharging their rifles at point-blank range, slashing at reins and leathers, driving home with their heavy spears, seeking at all costs to disable the horses and to drag down the riders. The cavalry, for their part, fought back with pistol, sword and lance, chopping and battering their way through the enemy ranks. And yet the whole thing was done by reflex, there was no time to gather one's wits, to look about one, even a second of hesitation and one was lost. 'The whole scene flickered exactly like a cinematograph picture,' noted Churchill. '. . . I remember no sound. The yells of the enemy, the shouts of the soldiers, the firing of many shots, the clashing of sword and spear, were unnoticed by the senses, unregistered by the brain. Perhaps it is possible for the whole of a man's faculties to be concentrated in the eye, bridle-hand, and trigger-finger, and withdrawn from all other parts of the body.'

Some Lancers had a harder time of it than others. Lt Grenfell's troop fared worst of all. They went into the khor at a place where they had to scale a high bank of boulders if they were to escape. Incredibly most of them succeeded but ten did not and eleven more were severely wounded. Robert Grenfell himself, scion of a great military family and *beau idéal* of the youthful cavalry officer, was first into the fight and first to fall. A sword took him in the back as, dismounted, he stumbled towards his horse. A spear thrust finished the business; another pierced his wrist, transfixing it and striking the watch so that the moment of his end was fixed for posterity. When his helmet was later found it was chopped almost to pieces with eleven cuts and thrusts marked on its surface. Lt Montmorency, of the next troop, with a courage which makes praise impertinent, turned back in search of a missing troop-sergeant into the hell through which he had fought his way. Instead he stumbled on the bleeding body of his friend. Somehow he managed to haul it on to his horse but the animal then bolted. Montmorency, armed only with a revolver, found himself abandoned in the midst of the screaming horde of dervishes. He could hardly have survived even a few seconds. Captain Kenna saw his plight and fought his way to his side, Corporal Swarbrick caught the terrified horse as it struggled to escape from the khor and dragged it back to its master. Though none of the three men could afterwards explain how they did it, somehow they hacked their way through the enemy to safety. Montmorency and Kenna were both rewarded with the Victoria Cross; Swarbrick, for reasons no doubt apparent to the dignitaries of the War Office, had to be content with the Distinguished Service Medal.

Lt Molyneux had an easier line of escape but it served him little when his horse collapsed dead under him. He set out for safety on foot but was quickly attacked by a group of dervishes. A blow from a sword disabled his right hand and his pistol fell to the ground. In another minute he would have been dead. Then he saw Private

Colonel Martin leading the charge of the 21st Lancers

Byrne a few yards away, his right arm hanging uselessly from a bullet wound, his chest bleeding from a spear thrust, but still mounted and active. Byrne was an Irishman, a somewhat disreputable member of Molyneux's troop who was notorious for his habit of smoking a short pipe on every occasion, especially when there was any prospect of action. In this he persisted in spite of every kind of reprimand and punishment. Now, with a cheerful, 'All right, sir. I won't leave you,' he battered his way over to his officer and held the dervishes at bay by lunging at them with his horse. His courage cost him dear. A spear thrust shaved his face. '—— the ——! He's broken my pipe,' exclaimed Private Byrne, a display of emotion which had not been won from him by either of his previous wounds. Meanwhile Molyneux tottered to safety, Byrne following as soon as he saw that the officer was safely away.

There were many such near-miraculous escapes. Captain Fair's sword snapped when he struck at a dervish lance and he only escaped by flinging the hilt into his adversary's face. Lt Wormald, in similar straits, found his sword bent double but fought his way out with it to keep it as a trophy. Lt Nesham, within a few feet of the edge of the khor and safety, had his bridle hand almost severed from his body. Then they were on him from every side. His helmet was cut through, his right leg deeply wounded, his right shoulder pierced. Two dervishes seized his legs to pull down what was now almost a helpless hulk and, as they did so, drove the spurs into the horse's body. The animal gave a prodigious heave forward and tore itself from their grasp; Nesham somehow retaining his seat and thus escaping. Colonel Martin rode right through without drawing sword or pistol; no doubt he had other things on his mind. Churchill, too, had a relatively easy passage: 'Opposite me they were about four deep. But they all fell knocked arse over tip and we passed through without any sort of shock.'

Lt Smyth's account of his passage could hardly have been bettered by Mr Jingle, yet in its breathless urgency it catches well the flavour of the adventure. 'Find myself at khor. Man bolts out leaving two donkeys in my way, catch hold of horse hard by head, knowing to fall would be fatal. He blunders against donkey, recovers and scrambles out, am met by swordsmen on foot, cuts at my right front, I guard it with sword. Next man, and a face all in white, having fired and missed me throws up both hands. I cut him across both hands, cuts at me, think this time I must be done but pace tells and my guard carries it off. Duck my head to spear thrown, just misses me, another cut at my horse, miss guard but luckily cut is too far away and only cuts through my breastplate and gives my horse a small flesh wound in the neck and shoulder. Then I remember no more till I find myself outside with 4 or 5 of my troop.'

They gave as good as they got. When a Seaforth officer inspected the khor two or three hours later he counted twenty-one dervish dead and two new graves. One of the graves belonged to the Emir Khalil who had been sitting on a fine black Dongolawi horse when a trooper drove a lance through his body and killed him instantly. There were twenty-one dead among the Lancers but sixty-five more seriously wounded and well over a quarter of the horses killed or maimed.

Lt McNeill of the Seaforths had been out on an errand for General Gatacre when he 'noticed a great commotion going on about a mile away to the south of Surgham. Crackling rifle fire, unmistakable British cheers and high clouds of dust'. He went over to investigate. 'The khor was full of dead and wounded dervishes and cavalry troop horses, and we could see the 21st Lancers reforming on the far side. We had to clear out pretty quick, as several troops dismounted and opened fire into the khor.'

Considering what they had gone through, the Lancers did indeed rally with impressive speed. Grenfell's troop sergeant had been so slashed by dervish swords that his nose and cheeks flapped hideously, his eyes were covered by streaming blood and he could hardly make himself heard for the blood pouring thickly down into his mouth. 'Rally, No. 2,' he tried to yell, reeling in his saddle. 'Fall out, sergeant, you're wounded!' called an officer from another troop. 'No, no, sir! Fall in! Fall in No. 2. Where are the devils? Show me the devils!' And so Grenfell's troop fell in – the four men who were still able to ride a horse.

'Horrible sights,' wrote Smyth. 'Everyone seems to be bleeding including my own horse. It seems to be blood, blood, blood everywhere. Horses and men smothered.'

Lieutenant de Montmorency and his Sergeant-Major after the charge

Churchill was in a characteristically pugnacious mood. 'I was quite clear then,' he told his mother, 'that we should have charged back at once . . . British cavalry so rarely get a chance that they must aim at the magnificent rather than the practical – and another 50 or 60 casualties would have made the performance historic – and have made us all proud of our race and blood. Never were soldiers more willing. I told my troop they were the finest men in the world and I am sure they would have followed me as far as I would have gone, and that I may tell you, and you only, was a very long way – for my soul becomes very high in such moments.'

Mercifully for the fifty or sixty Lancers whom Churchill was prepared to sacrifice so blithely on the altar of military glory, Colonel Martin decided that his men had had enough. The important thing was to drive the enemy from the khor. The Lancers galloped round to the dervish flank, dismounted and opened fire. The dervishes, who had survived their gruelling experience in quite as good order as the cavalry, wheeled to face them and began to advance. The fire they met, however, was too fast and accurate; they had hardly moved more than a few yards towards the cavalry before there was a change of plan, the line turned, and the dervishes moved back behind the Jebel Surgham. The Lancers, for what it was worth, were left in possession of the field. By the time they had inspected their dead, sent off their wounded to hospital and licked their wounds it was 9.30 a.m. and the rest of the army was hard at work elsewhere.

McNeill had by this time rejoined the main force, but the first inkling which most of his comrades had of the action came when 'there came cantering back to meet us a riderless white horse with his saddle and flanks literally drenched with blood'. Kitchener had already sent out an A.D.C. to find out what was going on and in a few minutes he galloped back with the news. Bagot with the Grenadiers called out to know what had happened. 'The 21st Lancers have caught it hot!' was the terse reply. The more details the Sirdar was given of the charge, the more indignant he became. Not only had the Lancers failed to give him any warning of the existence of Yakub's army – whose presence he was now discovering painfully for himself – but they had disqualified themselves from their even more important role of harrying the fugitives and, above all, making sure that the Khalifa did not escape. They should have avoided any serious action, above all one in which they lost more men in their own ranks than were killed among the enemies. 'It neither frightened nor hurt the dervishes much,' summed up a'Court, 'and it practically ruined the Lancers.'

Whether he relished it or not, however, the Sirdar was saddled with a group of popular heroes. In the climate of the day it was impossible to do anything except praise their exploit, albeit with as bad a grace as possible. He scarcely mentioned the incident in his official despatch and, though he paid the Lancers the compliment of going to see them off when they set sail down the Nile, there was little enthusiasm in his farewell address to them. 'I give a verbatim report of his speech,' wrote Churchill drily, 'since it tends to show that he is a man of deeds.'

For the British people, so cool an assessment of the action would have seemed irrelevant, almost blasphemous. The Lancers were the true heroes of Omdurman. Whatever one's opinion of their commanding officer it is hard not to feel that the judgment was a fair one. For gallantry and self-sacrifice their charge was of the highest order. Above all one's respect goes out not so much to the firebrand officers in search of glory as to the non-commissioned officers and the troopers who did what they had to do as a job of work and for a few shillings a week. After the dust had settled Churchill asked his second sergeant if he had enjoyed himself. 'Well, I don't exactly say I enjoyed it, Sir,' was the phlegmatic answer, 'but I think I'll get more used to it next time.' It was the spirit which won Waterloo and which was to carry the British soldiers through the hell of Flanders a mere sixteen years later.

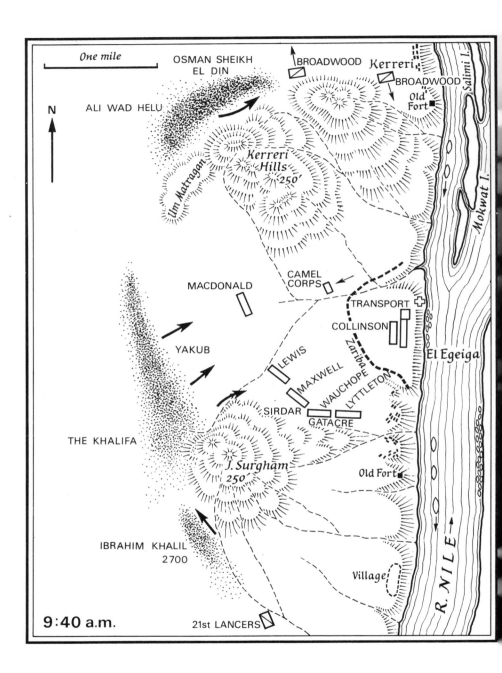

CHAPTER X

Macdonald's Brigade Stands Firm

A T about 9 a.m., half an hour or so after the Lancers had left on their ill-fated mission, the army set out on what was to be its final march. 'The excitement was intense,' said Bagot, as the Guards began to fall in outside their zariba, 'and the intensity showed itself in that curious stillness which always marks anything really out of the common and when real business is meant.' Bagot himself had already suffered a painful wound in the right arm but this was not going to hold him back now that what must be the kill was at last in sight.

Already some people had been given a taste of what was in store for them. Like casual sightseers they had strayed out in front of the lines to take a look at the dead and collect a few souvenirs. Four camp servants went 300 yards or so ahead of Maxwell's 2nd Brigade. Suddenly, from the stony soil, a 'dead' dervish, blood-stained and limping, rose and charged them with a spear. They turned and fled towards the zariba while a Sudanese corporal who was with them dropped on to one knee and fired. His Martini-Henry missed fire. He fired again. This time the shot went wide and the corporal, awed by the horrific figure bearing down on him, scuttled away to safety. One of the war correspondents, also surveying the scene, now found himself the target. He waited calmly until the dervish was a mere twenty paces away, cocked his four-barrelled Lancaster pistol, aimed with great deliberation, fired, missed, and joined the growing group of fugitives.

Bennet Burleigh of the *Daily Telegraph*, seeing his colleague in such straits, rode towards the dervish, fired, scored a hit, fired again, missed, and, judging that he had done his bit, rode rapidly away. One of the Sirdar's A.D.C.s, Lt Smith of the Grenadiers, galloped up to finish off the job. He rode at the dervish who, by this time, was tottering on his feet, fired and missed. Wheeling his horse he collided with the dervish who, with a final despairing effort, grabbed Smith and drove his spear at him. He could do no more than scrape the English officer's arm. Smith raised his revolver and, holding it so that it almost touched the dervish's head, at last applied the *coup de grâce*. The butchery had been neither elegant nor efficient, if every dervish casualty was going to cause the same amount of trouble then it was evident that the army was in for an exacting march.

If Kitchener had used the same formation in the advance as he had done within the zariba, Collinson's 4th Egyptian Brigade would have been on the right and in the rear, advancing at the foot of the Kerreri hills and well to the right of the Jebel Surgham. General Hunter, however, was nervous about the presence of this untried brigade on the exposed flank. The force under Ali Wad Helu which had swept in front of the Egeiga encampment must still be in existence somewhere and even though there was reason to suppose that it had let itself be diverted into a futile pursuit of the cavalry, it must eventually come to its senses and return to the battle. Macdonald's predominantly Sudanese Ist Brigade was selected for the doubtful privilege of dealing with it if it did re-appear. Otherwise the order of advance was as it had been in defence. The two British brigades advanced towards the ridge which ran between the Jebel Surgham and the river. Maxwell's and Lewis's brigades headed more or less directly for the Jebel Surgham itself, on whose crest it was suspected that the Khalifa himself might be ensconced with a small but still formid-able force. Collinson's Egyptian brigade was given the humble task of escorting the transport along the banks of the Nile. With such a disposition it was inevitable that Macdonald was going to find himself to some extent isolated as he marched between the Jebel Surgham and the Kerreri hills. To help him he was reinforced by three batteries of field artillery and a battery of maxims; sufficient fire-power, it was hoped, to sustain him against any enemy that might swoop down.

Captain Douglas Haig of the Egyptian cavalry angrily criticized the Sirdar's tactics. The proper thing for Kitchener to have done, he maintained, would have been to throw his left flank forward to the Jebel Surgham and then draw in his right and gradually extend his left south-wards so as to cut off the enemy from Omdurman. Instead he spread out his force and left one section of it dangerously exposed. 'He seems to have had no plan, or tactical idea, for beating the enemy beyond allowing the latter to attack the camp. . . . Having six brigades, is it tactics to fight a very superior enemy with one of them and to keep the others beyond supporting distance? To me it seems truly fortunate that the *flower* of the dervish army exhausted itself first in an attack and pursuit of the cavalry. Indeed, the prisoners say: "You would never have defeated us had you not *deceived* us." '

Haig was being wise after the event, but the results of Kitchener's tactics were very much as he stated them. The *intention*, however, was quite different. Macdonald's brigade was never meant to be 'beyond supporting dis-tance' of the rest of the army. If the five brigades in the main advance had kept their distance all would have been relatively well. But they did not and, given the country over which they were advancing and the state of their training, there was never any real hope that they would. 'What Kitchener then needed,' commented a'Court, 'was a good infantry drill man, and he did not have one.'

The trouble started with the British brigades. The 2nd brigade was given pride of place in the advance. The officers and men of the 1st British brigade were indignant at what seemed to them a most unfair piece of favouritism. No distance had been fixed between one unit and another so they made the best of a bad job by marching virtually on the heels of their rivals. A'Court was sent galloping back to protest. 'You don't think we are going to let you enter Omdurman before us, do you?' was the brisk retort. The sentiment was perhaps natural in the circumstances but not likely to lead to a particularly well-ordered advance. With the British division thus rushing helter skelter towards Omdurman, the two Egyptian brigades nearer to it put on all speed to keep themselves in contact with the leaders. The luckless Macdonald, as he moved the 1st Egyptian brigade out into the desert to take its proper place in the echelon, thus found himself without a friend in sight and surrounded by an alarming amount of country from which a waiting enemy might emerge.

Whatever forebodings the 1st Brigade might have had, the mood of the rest of the army was one of jubilation. John Ewart was with the first group of the Camerons to breast the ridge between the Jebel Surgham and the Nile. 'Many of us felt like the great Napoleon's veterans when they got their first glimpse of Moscow in 1812. Before us lay Omdurman and Khartoum. Conspicuous in the centre of the vast city of mud houses rose the dome of the Mahdi's tomb; its weathercock, or whatever may have stood for one, gone, and a huge gap in its white roof. It was a refreshing sight, calculated to make one feel cool and to forget the joys of bully-beef.' Though sniping fire from the top of the Jebel was becoming more frequent and was beginning to cause Maxwell's brigade a certain amount of irritation, the scene was still a relatively peaceful one and there was little to mar the euphoria of the advancing troops.

Then heavy and continuous rifle fire was heard from the desert to the north of the Jebel Surgham. Almost immediately a field gun joined in the fusillade. 'Hello,' said the Sirdar. 'That must be Mac!' The battle was on again. About half an hour before this Macdonald had seen what looked like a considerable force of dervishes on the western slopes of the Jebel. Though the full mass of the army of the black flag was still sheltered from his view, enough was visible to make it obvious that his flank would be in danger if he advanced much further. Lt Pritchard of the Engineers was sent posting across to the next brigade in line to ask for help in an attack on this new enemy. Taffy Lewis, the brigade commander, was a brave and energetic man, but it was not in his nature to challenge orders. Kitchener had just sent him a peremptory instruction to close the gap between his brigade and Maxwell's; to ignore this and march off in the opposite direction was unthinkable. Pritchard was given short shrift and, to Macdonald's dismay, the 3rd Brigade continued on its way and shortly disappeared behind the mountain. Lewis was 'a gallant little chap', said his adjutant, Captain Sparks, fondly but patronisingly, 'but I think he now lost the chance of his life'.

No one could blame Lewis for his decision. The Sirdar's judgment is more open to question. After his rebuff from Lewis, Macdonald sent the unfortunate Pritchard galloping back over the slopes of the Jebel to where Kitchener and his staff were advancing behind Maxwell's brigade. Pritchard explained that what was clearly a very considerable force of dervishes lay hidden over the mountain. Was Macdonald to attack it? And could Lewis's brigade lend a hand? 'Cannot Colonel Macdonald see that we are marching on Omdurman?' was the lofty reply. 'Tell him to follow on.' No subaltern – except possibly Winston Churchill – is likely to relish arguing with his Commander-in-Chief but Pritchard did his best. It seemed to gain him nothing and in a moment he was on his way back to Macdonald with the dustiest of dusty answers. Yet he had done better than he knew. Beneath his stolid, almost bovine countenance Kitchener was a prey to considerable doubts; it only needed the sound of heavy firing to convince him that he had made a bad mistake.

From the vantage point to which he quickly galloped he saw that Macdonald had deployed his force and opened fire; the enemy were as yet hardly to be seen but already the first banners were becoming visible not much more than 800 yards from Macdonald's line. Steevens of the *Daily Mail* decided his duty lay where the action was and, with another journalist, galloped behind the lines of the 1st Brigade. They found Macdonald dismounted and walking about, 'very gleeful in his usual grim way'. 'Gentlemen,' he greeted the new arrivals, 'I am delighted to welcome you and I think I can show you some good sport.'

The sport had already begun. At the sight of a new dervish army bearing down on them, apparently as large as that which had recently assaulted the entire army at El Egeiga, the Sudanese troops became almost hysterical with excitement. At first it seemed that nothing could stop them leaving their line and charging the enemy, a movement which could only have led to their annihilation. The officers eventually managed to check this suicidal urge, but could not prevent their men opening fire independently and long before the enemy were close enough to offer any chance of success. Macdonald realised that safety was only to be found in perfect discipline. With his brigade major, a trumpeter and the unwearying Pritchard he rode down the front of the line, knocking up his men's rifles and shouting to them to cease fire. As the dervishes grew near their fire began to get uncomfortably accurate, from the Anglo-Egyptian ranks an occasional bullet whipped within inches of the colonel and his party. Macdonald was indifferent to the danger from whatever source it came. Such conduct would have been brave from anyone, from Macdonald it was doubly so. Only a few days before he had heard a Sudanese private abusing him and threatening to shoot him in the back. Calmly he had walked up to him, ordered him to load his rifle and had then turned his back. The man had fallen to his knees and prayed for mercy, there had been no further signs of discontent. Yet the memory of the incident must still have been vivid in the colonel's mind. His heroism was rewarded. For two minutes – which seemed to Pritchard the longest two minutes he had ever or would ever pass – Macdonald harangued his men; reminding them of their training and of what was expected of them. When he rode back inside the line, complete calm and order reigned.

By now the dervishes were within four hundred yards. There they checked, while Yakub, who would not let any infidel outmatch him in courage, in turn rode out in front of his men and urged them to a special effort. The dervish charge and the first volley from the defenders came almost simultaneously. Fifteen thousand fighting men, the pick of the dervish armies, bore down upon the 1st brigade. A detachment from the Khalifa's bodyguard was at their heels. Babikr Bedri was standing behind the black flag, watching as the gap between Macdonald's men and the dervish army inexorably narrowed. 'When we saw them like moving yellow cliffs,' he recorded, 'the Khalifa called to the officers of the Guard, "*Abjakka*! Up! Lead your comrades to repulse these enemies of God!" The Reinforcement Guard leapt up, and we saw them advance about a hundred metres or a little more, firing at intervals, and the enemy fired on them with a sound like "Runnnn!" They did not return.' 'So rapid was our fire,' said Pritchard, 'that above the sound of the explosions could be heard the swish of our bullets going through the air just like the swish of water.'

The wave of sound rolled over the desert to Omdurman

and was heard by Neufeld as he crouched in chains in the Khalifa's prison. Was this the storming of the zariba? Or a final attack on the Khalifa? He hardly dared to speculate. By now one or two survivors of the first assault had limped into the city. Neufeld operated on one with a penknife to extract a bullet from the temple. 'Bodily pain, as we understand it, is unknown to them,' he commented complacently. But at least he got from his patient the news that one onslaught on the expeditionary force had failed.

There were plenty more casualties who could now have done with medical treatment, but still they came on. By this time the leading dervishes were within a hundred yards of Macdonald's line and, as each one fell, another was immediately behind him to carry the advance a few yards further. One emir was hit twice, reeled in his saddle but, as if he knew that death was coming and was determined to meet it like a man, galloped at full speed towards the enemy. His spear was raised to throw when a bullet plucked him from his horse, 'exactly as if he had been knocked off by the branch of a tree'. Still they came nearer; it seemed that within only a few moments the two lines must fuse into the carnage of hand-to-hand conflict.

Meanwhile, however, the Sirdar hurriedly revised his tactics. For the moment the march on Omdurman was abandoned. Maxwell was ordered to storm the heights of the Jebel Surgham and take Macdonald's attackers in the flank. Lyttelton, with the 2nd British brigade, took position on Maxwell's left and Lewis on his right while Wauchope, with the 1st British brigade, hastened across the desert to fill the gap which had been left between Lewis and Macdonald. The result of this manoeuvre was that the army changed front and Yakub's mighty force bearing down upon its prey found itself suddenly attacked from the side by the fire of three new brigades. The operation, sensibly conceived and swiftly carried out, showed the Sirdar at his best, yet also vividly illustrated

Colonel Macdonald's brigade repel an attack

what could at times be his greatest weakness. 'He ran the show absolutely off his own bat,' commented his brother Walter. 'His staff were not given the chance of remembering the most ordinary details.'

For Macdonald the relief was immediate. The long line of allied infantry advancing down the slopes of the Jebel Surgham forced Yakub to switch large bodies of men to confront the new menace. There was a moment of peril for Kitchener's army when the 7th Egyptians, the battalion on the extreme right of Lewis's brigade, began to waver and retreat in the face of the dervish attack. Here, where there was still a gaping hole in the allied line, was the point of greatest danger. Quickly the 15th Egyptians, with fixed bayonets, marched up behind their compatriots. The line steadied, the advance went on.

Suddenly it was no longer Yakub's army which was dictating the course of events. Instead he found himself contained within the two strokes of a great V. Macdonald still stood firm while, every moment, the fire from the reinforcements coming in on Yakub's left flank became more fearful. Lewis's 3rd brigade alone fired more than 37,000 rounds. The maxims too were doing heavy damage. An enterprising engineer subaltern, Lt R. B. Blakeney, had hoisted a couple of maxims to the very summit of the Jebel and was directing withering blasts of fire at the dervish masses. It was more than the most heroic could support. Yakub's army began to falter and retreat into the desert; away from Macdonald and away from Omdurman.

The Khalifa was watching from a small knoll a few hundred yards from the fighting. As he watched Yakub rallying his troops a shell pitched almost at his brother's feet, tossing him and his bodyguard in broken fragments high into the air. The Khalifa cared more for Yakub than any other member of his family as well as having the most touching confidence in his prowess as a warrior. For the first time he began to lose hope. From the group around him a blind emir edged his horse outwards, towards the sound of the firing. It was the brother of Ibrahim al Khalil killed in the charge of the 21st Lancers. Now the blind man's beloved commander had followed his brother to paradise. He had already lived too long. A man pointed his horse towards Macdonald's lines, another struck its rump with the side of his sword. Solitary, the sightless warrior began his last charge; solitary he checked, reeled and fell. One more hero joined the mountain of the dead.

The Khalifa dismounted and knelt upon his prayer skin, surrounded by a six-deep wall of his bodyguard. Surely the Prophet and the Mahdi would offer guidance on what was to be done? As he prostrated himself, the Emir Said al-Makki burst through the ranks and shook him by the shoulder. 'Why do you sit here?' he expostulated. 'So long as you are alive religion is victorious. Escape! Everyone is being killed.' Another Emir, Al Baana, was standing nearby. 'When I heard Said al-Makki say this and saw that the Khalifa did not protest, I got up and took hold of him under his armpits – a thing no man would have dared to do before – and raised him up.' At first the Khalifa refused to ride, but after falling three times on the rough ground, allowed himself to be persuaded on to a donkey. As he rode off, the men who had revered him a few hours before jeered at his progress: 'Where, oh Abdullahi, where is the victory you promised?' Though he did not know it, it was nearer than at any other moment of the battle.

For Macdonald was in great danger. From his perch on the Jebel, Blakeney had seen it coming a good fifteen minutes before. 'Macdonald's brigade was blazing away at a large force of the enemy, above whom fluttered a huge black flag; but away to the north, perhaps unseen by him though clearly visible to me, was another army of about 10,000 dervishes under a green flag.' It was the army of Sheikh el Din, returned at last from chasing Broadwood's cavalry over the Sudanese desert, with the 5500 men of Ali Wad Helu, who had been quietly biding their time in the fringes of the Kerreri hills. It was far worse than Blakeney had supposed: there were 20,000 of them at least, many of them as fresh as when they had started, all of them itching to get at the infidels and avenge their brothers. Now the full value of Broadwood's action in drawing away the bulk of the dervishes became apparent. If Sheikh el Din had got his forces back on to the battlefield even half an hour earlier, Macdonald and all his brigade would have been annihilated. Never could his Sudanese have resisted the simultaneous onslaught of two armies on his different flanks.

Even as it was the difficulties of the 1st Brigade were immense enough. Macdonald had been on the point of ordering a counter attack against the enfeebled forces of Yakub when Captain St G. Henry, an officer of the

Northumberland Fusiliers attached to the Camel Corps, galloped down with the news that an entirely new and still more formidable onslaught was about to begin. Instantly Macdonald revised his plans. Wholly unmoved by the growing danger and with the detached air of a drill sergeant expounding a complicated barrack-square manoeuvre to a group of learners, he called his battalion commanders together and scratched busily in the sand to demonstrate his intentions. Then he remounted, and one by one, began to pull his battalions out of the western front on to a new line confronting the menace to the north.

First to move were the XIth Sudanese. Though the pace of the battle was slackening they were still hectically engaged with Yakub's army when they left their first position; Sheikh el Din's vanguard was already within rifle range by the time they arrived at their new location. To turn one's back on an enemy while still under fire, double several hundred yards while preserving one's formation and resume the fight with a new enemy at the instant of arrival in a new position is an operation that would test the most experienced veterans. The XIth Sudanese, temporarily commanded by the indefatigable Pritchard, carried it out with an aplomb that could not have been surpassed by any regiment of the British army. Simultaneously half the IXth Sudanese and a battery of the artillery on the right of Macdonald's original line acted as pivot between the old and the new position, by swivelling on their ground so that they too faced the on-coming threat from the Kerreri hills. It was characteristic of Macdonald that, even in the heat of battle, he found time to summon the battalion officers and scold them for acting before they received their orders.

It was while the action was at its height that General Hunter, the divisional commander, decided to take a hand. Concluding that Macdonald's position was rapidly ap-proaching the desperate he sent an A.D.C. with instructions that the 1st Brigade was to withdraw if pressure continued to build up. Macdonald would have none of it. He knew that his Sudanese, staunch in standing their ground, would quickly become a disorganised rabble in retreat. 'I'll no do it. I'll see them damned first! We maun just fight,' he is said to have exclaimed. The identity of 'them' was unspecified; presumably it included a considerable number of dervishes as well as General Hunter. His one concession was to send the ever-willing Pritchard off to Wauchope to ask him to bring the 1st British Brigade up on his right, instead of on his left as had been the original intention. Wauchope expostulated that this was the opposite of what Hunter had ordered. His doubts did not last long. A glance at the battlefield, as he crested the rise between him and the action, convinced him that Macdonald's right did indeed need reinforcement. The Lincolns were despatched at the double to lend a hand.

It was almost too late. By now the other half of the IXth and the Xth Sudanese had been switched into the new positions but still the dervishes forced their way closer, pushing on with the unthinking heroism that their compatriots had shown at Egeiga, though this time with a fair chance of success. Macdonald himself remained imperturbable. His composure was the more remarkable because he was in severe pain from a kick which the horse belonging to one of his battalion commanders had landed on his leg just below the knee. For a moment he almost fainted but he quickly recovered, felt his leg to ensure nothing was broken and calmly carried on. All around him men were suffering more serious blows; there were more than 120 casualties in the 1st Brigade in less than twenty minutes. Shortly after 10 a.m. the dervishes had got to within a hundred yards of the Xth Sudanese. Morale among the defenders was high but under this savage pressure the shooting was growing wild. The officers rushed from man to man, pleading with them by name,

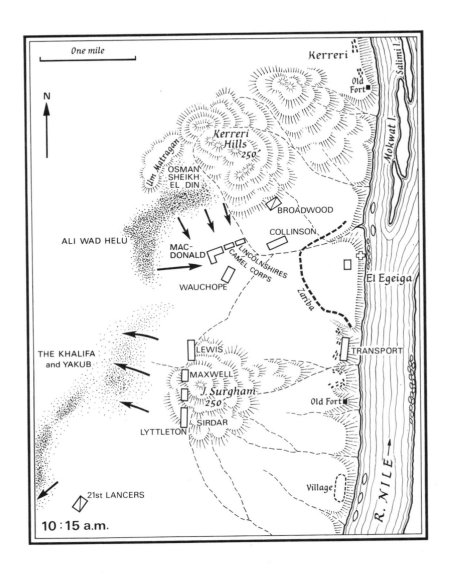

One mile

N

Kerreri

Salimi I.

Old
Fort■

Mokwat I.

Kerreri
Hills
250'

Um Matragan

OSMAN
SHEIKH
EL DIN

BROADWOOD

ALI WAD HELU

MAC-
DONALD

COLLINSON

LINCOLNSHIRES

CAMEL CORPS

El Egeiga

WAUCHOPE

Zariba

THE KHALIFA
and YAKUB

LEWIS

TRANSPORT

MAXWELL

J. Surgham
250'

Old Fort■

SIRDAR

LYTTLETON

Village

21st LANCERS

R. NILE

10:15 a.m.

themselves seizing the rifles and adjusting the sights. It
served no purpose, still the hectic and wasteful fire went
on.

The dervishes were within fifty, forty yards. The artillery and the maxim guns were still blasting holes in the
advancing line but the infantry were running out of

ammunition. Not more than half a dozen rounds a man were left. Thirty yards, and the Sudanese braced themselves for the clash. It was the moment at which an advancing enemy becomes an individual, a personal and urgent threat; at which a distant and unreal menace is suddenly translated into the likelihood of imminent death. Twenty yards, and the reserves of ammunition had dwindled still further. Macdonald's Sudanese knew that they were outnumbered by at least ten to one but arithmetic counted for nothing in the fierce joy of battle. Ten yards, and the foremost enemy were hurling their spears into the allied lines, dervishes were dying almost at the end of the rifle barrel. As A Company of the Lincolnshires breasted the rise that hid the fighting, Lt Hodgson thought for an instant that help had come too late, that Macdonald's line had been broken and the 1st Egyptian Brigade would soon be wholly overrun. Then he saw that the two forces were still divided by a few yards of blood-stained sand, that the Xth Sudanese had held their ground and were poised, bayonets ready, for the shock of the dervish onslaught.

The Lincolnshires were the 10th of Foot, and they had adopted the Xth Sudanese as an honorary black battalion; a detail which gave added pleasure to both the rescuers and the rescued. They also had a reputation as the fastest and most accurate firers of volleys in the British army. As each company came up into line, to the right of the Sudanese and at an angle to it so that they took the attackers in the flank, they put their claim to the test. The first volley blasted a gap between the defenders and the advancing dervishes; then, as company after company joined in the firing, the foremost enemy were time and again cut down. Struck by this sudden menace from their flank the attack faltered. Some of the dervishes turned and hurled themselves hopelessly towards the Lincolns, others stood as if bemused, unable to accept that their prey had suddenly been snatched away.

Now three more battalions of artillery joined in from behind the right wing of the allied line and the shells began to fall, each one leaving a pool of dead and wounded which stood empty for a moment before the dervishes milled forward once again over the bodies of their fellows. Exultantly Macdonald's brigade prepared to advance on their now demoralised foe. And then came the *coup de grâce*. Over the crest of the hill to the right came the rest of the 1st British Brigade: the Seaforths, the Camerons and the Warwicks. Egerton of the Seaforths was one of the first to view the battlefield. He saw the dense mass of the dervishes already faltering and ebbing to and fro like an angry sea, the long line of Macdonald's brigade poised to counter-attack, the Lincolns on the right firing section-volleys with disciplined precision and shattering effect. . . . 'the unexpected appearance of our long line of some 3000 white faces topping the hill changed the situation at once; the attack ceased and broke . . .'

In ten minutes the situation had been transformed; from triumphant attack the dervishes now found themselves outflanked to right and left. To advance was impossible, to remain where they were meant certain destruction, they turned and ran. The mounted emirs tried desperately to check the rout but it was too late. Within a few minutes all that remained was a group of about 500 Baggara horsemen clustered around the standard of Ali Wad Helu. Egerton waited, expecting to see them gallop off behind the wreckage of their army. Instead they turned and charged; hurling themselves in hopeless defiance at Macdonald's line. Here indeed was the flower of dervish chivalry; knowing that all hope of victory had gone but preferring to die in glory rather than to quit the battlefield in defeat. To Vandeleur, watching behind the ranks of the 3rd Brigade, they rode as if it was the finish of the Derby, each man intent on one thing only, to reach the line before his fellows. They had no chance, of course.

The fight for the Khalifa's black flag

They began their charge from 500 yards; by the time they had covered half the distance less than 200 remained mounted, at 100 yards barely a score survived. Captain Sparks drew his pistol and fired once as the last dervish came within twenty yards of the line, but the effort was unnecessary, the man was dead before the bullet found him. 'It was one of the finest things I've ever seen,' recorded Sparks in wonder. 'Not one man faltered, each rode to his death without flinching.'

177

Of course not all the dervishes were heroes. Babikr Bedri and his fellow doubters had watched appalled as the first casualties began to totter back. This was not at all what they had planned. 'We noticed that for every wounded man there were four others carrying or supporting him; so I said to our little group, "Look here, if one of us gets wounded I shall get wounded too – with his blood, and the rest of you can carry us away . . ." ' At last the dreaded moment came when Muhammad, one of the Mahdi's sons, ordered an advance. Bedri had noticed a little hillock of sand which lay ahead and he and his friends scuttled anxiously towards it 'and watched the flag fall and rise again, fall and rise again, and at the third fall the hail of bullets thickened about us'. They cowered thus for a few minutes, their heads almost literally buried in the sand, indifferent to the outcome of the battle but wishing only that it would go away. 'Then Mustafa, the man on my right, received a wound in the left hand, and I came to my senses at last. I slipped off my turban, smeared it in my neighbour's blood, and bound it on my left arm; then I called to my companions, "Now two of us are wounded!" They jumped up from cover, and four of them carried back each one of us and we got away.' The genuine casualty soon found that the danger was not being quickly enough left behind and clamoured to be put down. With some reluctance the bearers put down their precious alibi, 'and as soon as he was free of us he ran faster than we did, and by God we couldn't catch him up!'

The charge was over, the last horse careering riderless away. Now Macdonald could order an advance, driving the shattered dervish rabble back into the Kerreri hills from whence they had come. From behind the line Kitchener turned to his staff. 'I think we've given them a good dusting, gentlemen!' and he slammed his glasses shut with a gesture of satisfaction. It was 11.30 a.m., high

178

time to regroup the army and get back onto the road to Omdurman.

It is hard to see that he had any personal grounds for complacency. He had exposed Macdonald's men to an unnecessary and unacceptable risk and it was no thanks to him that the 1st Egyptian Brigade had not been totally destroyed. The valour of the men, the skill of the commander, had saved the day. Felix Ready had rejoined the main army and was with Macdonald throughout the battle. 'Our battalion has done so well it has become the talk of the whole Egyptian army,' he proudly proclaimed. 'Whatever anyone says about the other brigades the brunt of the whole fight was borne by us for four hours. We went from 4 a.m. till 10.30 p.m. with only a cold sausage and a cup of cocoa at 4.30 a.m. . . . and in the saddle from 7 a.m. till 4 p.m. A longish day, but I wouldn't have missed it for the world.' It was still asking too much of the men. 'A bad business,' said Haig grumpily, and a bad business it remained, however much Macdonald might have turned it into victory. Over-confidence cannot lightly be condoned in the commanders of great armies. But victory it was; and as the shattered remnants of Sheikh el Din's once glorious army fled towards the Kerreri hills it became clear that it was something near to final victory. What would be found when the troops reached Omdurman itself was still a mystery but between the city and the allies nothing remained but the dead, the maimed and the despairing fugitives.

CHAPTER XI

To the Walls of the Citadel

FOR the Khalifa it seemed like the end of everything. In the space of a few hours he had tumbled abjectly from demi-god to less than human; betrayer of his family, his people, his faith. But all was not irrevocably lost. Though the dead and dying strewed the plain about him there were many thousands who were fit to fight. It was still within his power to fall back on Omdurman and do what he should have done in the first place, turn every house into a fortress and make the infidel pay in blood for every step he took within the city confines. Meanwhile, his own dependants must be looked after. He called his camel syce, Abou Gekka, and told him to hurry ahead to Omdurman and collect wives, children and treasure on the parade ground in front of his house. Then he saw Yakub's devoted eunuch servant in the throng and ordered him to do the same for his master's property. 'Where is *my* master?' asked the eunuch with some effrontery. The Khalifa's frail grasp on his self-control snapped instantly. 'Who is this slave to question my orders?' he screamed, and a few seconds later the eunuch lay dead at his feet.

As the Khalifa and his bodyguard began to leave the field, Wingate, standing on a knoll some 2000 yards away, spotted that some movement of importance was going on. Through his glasses he identified the dervish leader and quickly ordered Major Williams, whose battery was nearby, to open fire. The first shot went wide but the second fell only a few yards in front of the cortège. It was a good shot; too good, in fact, for it galvanised the group of dervishes into a gallop. The next round fell precisely where

180

Sudanese looting after the battle

the Khalifa would have been if he had continued at the same pace, as it was it killed half a dozen dervishes at the tail of the escort. The little band vanished from sight; the Khalifa curiously heartened by his narrow escape which seemed to him evidence that Allah had not yet deserted him.

Kitchener had no doubt what the enemy intended, nor any illusions about the dangers and difficulties he would face if Omdurman were strongly garrisoned. The time lost rescuing Macdonald meant that it was too late now for the infantry to reach Omdurman before the bulk of the fugitives but the cavalry could still do something to check the flow. On the left the 21st Lancers probed deep across the plain. Many of the dervishes, at their approach, flung down their weapons, held up their hands and pleaded for mercy; droves of prisoners were escorted towards the Nile. Many, however, while anxious to avoid a fight, were still more anxious to escape without the indignity of surrender. In their thousands they flowed across the plain; 'just like the people hurrying into Newmarket town after the Cambridgeshire', as one prosaic officer remarked. The handful of Lancers could hardly hope to check this multitude but they could at least do something to ensure that Newmarket was never reached. By harrassing them from the flank, or by dismounting and firing occasional volleys into their midst, they drove the dervishes farther out into the desert so that the main link of retreat was no longer directed at the city but far into the plains to the north.

On the right wing Broadwood and the Egyptian cavalry had a tougher task. As soon as it had become clear that Sheikh el Din's attack was broken and his army falling back into the Kerreri hills Broadwood was sent to harry what was left of Yakub's forces and head them off from Omdurman. 'We were formed into two lines,' recorded Capt Legge of the 20th Hussars, a veteran of the whole campaign who had been wounded at Firket and was now acting as Brigade Major, 'and galloped for four miles without a check after the retreating dervishes'. Then the cavalry wheeled to the left, towards Omdurman. Though shot at repeatedly, sometimes by large bands of fugitives, they never drew rein but sabred or lanced any dervish within range who showed signs of fight. They took more than 1000 prisoners, breaking the rifles of those who had any and sending them back towards the Sirdar. But as they got nearer the city the going grew steadily harder. 'We came across a large body of dervishes full of "buck". Four squadrons went for them, charged straight through them, wheeled and charged again.' Colonel Broadwood then appeared with the rest of the cavalry and the demoralised enemy broke and ran.

They left the dead in piles behind them but casualties

183

among the cavalry had not been light. Ahead, to the north of the city, the retreating enemy were concentrated still more heavily. To advance further would have been to court heavy loss and to gain little, since already Yakub's army was pulling to the south and west, away from Omdurman. Broadwood reckoned that one head thrust into a hornet's nest had been enough. To the dismay of some but the relief of most, he wheeled and led his cavalry across the plain to join up with the Sirdar on the outskirts of the city.

Meanwhile the infantry had regrouped and resumed its advance. Even to the most hardened veterans of the slaughterhouse, the battlefield was a spectacle it would be hard ever to forget. The dead lay so thick that in parts the ground was scarcely visible: 'some lay very composedly with their slippers placed under their heads for a last pillow, some knelt, cut short in the middle of a last prayer. Others were torn to pieces, vermilion blood already drying on brown skin, killed instantly beyond a doubt.' Nor were the dead more horrifying than the dying. 'One dervish raised his face to mine with a ghastly smile,' wrote Bennett for the *Westminster Gazette*, 'as if deprecating our violence, and throwing his gibbah on one side, displayed an awful wound. Another man lay face downward, breathing bubbles through a pool of gore, and actually drowning in his own blood.'

And everywhere there were the wounded: one nursing a shattered arm; another clutching his stomach, his intestines oozing horribly through his tensed fingers; a third holding an eye that was no longer an eye but a gaping, blackened hole around which the flies malevolently clustered. However grave their wounds their only thought was of water, their common destination the distant Nile. And so the luckier hobbled onwards, the less fortunate inched forward on their knees or crawled with stomach to the soil, leaving a trail of blood to mark their passing.

184

Many died, so great was their strength and fortitude that incredibly many survived, survived to reach the river, survived even to recover from their wounds. Corporal Emery of the Rifle Brigade had never believed that men could suffer pain so stoically: 'I saw one with his hand blown off, and his scalp half torn off sitting down and eating a biscuit quite calmly.'

A moment later he was jerked abruptly from his mood of contemplative pity. 'As I was walking over a mound of earth which raised me above the rest,' he wrote, 'I saw a wounded man lying about twenty yards off aim bang at me and fire: I heard the bullet whizz past my ear.' Almost at the same moment a private with the Seaforths, a few hundred yards away, suddenly saw a huge dervish, about 6 ft 4 ins tall, rise as from the dead. ' "Look out, chaps!" I shouted. His sword could have sliced off at least two of our heads in one sweep.' Four men closed in on the dervish and he fell pierced by bayonet thrusts from every direction. 'I shall never forget the look in his eyes as he dropped his heavy sword and fell. After that, if any dervish showed a flicker of life, he was disposed of because: "It's you or me, chum, and it's not going to be me!" '

There were quite enough instances of this nature to prove that the dervish wounded did indeed need to be treated with the gravest suspicion; but the attitude of the victorious allies still leaves a great deal to be desired. The war correspondent, Ernest Bennett, caused a furore when he wrote a piece in *Contemporary* accusing the British troops of slaughtering the wounded. As if this was not enough, he compounded his crime by asserting that this had become customary since Tel-el-Kebir. A particularly moving vignette in his article featured a Highlander brutally bayoneting a grey-beard who knelt before him begging for mercy. Bennett was one of the most disliked men in the Sudan and a note of petulant spite runs through all he wrote, but he was not totally a liar. Lt Fison of the

5th Fusiliers said categorically that, before the advance, 'the Sirdar had issued orders that all wounded passed over had to be bayoneted' while Winston Churchill wrote to his mother, 'I shall merely say that the victory at Omdurman was disgraced by the inhuman slaughter of the wounded and that Kitchener was responsible for this.'

It is hard to believe that Kitchener in fact gave any specific order of the kind to which Fison referred; apart from anything else he was far too cautious a man to court the damaging criticism which might have followed. Quite as many accounts testify to his readiness, even eagerness, to spare lives whenever the opportunity was given him. But at the very least it appears that he did not do enough positively to inhibit the unnecessary number of dervish wounded. It would, indeed, have been quite contrary to his temperament if he had. 'Thou shalt not kill, but need'st not strive officiously to keep alive.' Probably there were relatively few cases of out-and-out murder among the better disciplined British troops but the Sudanese accepted with relish the chance to pay off old scores and the camp-followers, the jackals who scavenge around the fringe of every army, were everywhere behind the advancing infantry, clubbing and stabbing the helpless wounded and fumbling in the clothes of the dead in search of trinkets to sell as souvenirs to the British troops. Many British officers condoned the slaughter. 'If I had had my way,' wrote Smyth of the Lancers, 'every man we captured on the battlefield should have been shot there and then, cold blood or not.'

Nor did the more exalted always set a good example. Lionel James of Reuters was riding with Slatin Pasha, hurrying to catch up with the Sirdar and his staff. They met a small boy leading a donkey on which sat a stout and imposing dervish, obviously in great pain. Slatin rode closer and recognised the man as the emir Osman Azrak. 'I have never seen the expression of a man's face change so magically,' wrote James. 'Slatin's expression became ferocious: he drew back his lips like a starving wolf.' For years as a prisoner of the Mahdi Slatin had suffered above all from Osman Azrak's malign brutality; now was the time for revenge. He said something to the boy who stopped the donkey with a jerk, sending its rider sprawling. Then Slatin gestured to a passing Sudanese soldier who, with satisfied alacrity, drew his bayonet and ran Osman Azrak several times through the body. Within a few seconds the great dervish leader lay dead.

James was a usually reliable correspondent. It is only fair to Slatin, however, to say that there was no other witness of this curious incident and that his leading biographer* believes that any such conduct would have been wholly out of character. Other authorities, also, maintain that Osman Azrak died in the first attack on El Egeiga several hours before. The verdict on Slatin must be not proven, perhaps not guilty, but the fact remains that a sober and decent war correspondent could describe the incident without any apparent realisation that it was anything out of the ordinary.

The Seaforths were one of the first British regiments to resume the march. Their course took them directly past the spot to which the Khalifa's banner had been carried in the vanguard of Yakub's attack. The great black flag flopped dismally from its pole which was still planted firmly in the sand. 'Round it,' noticed Egerton, 'lay a mass of white clad bodies, in appearance forming what might have been likened to a large white croquet ground or lawn tennis court outlined on the yellow sand.' The Sirdar and his staff rode up behind the Highlanders. Such wounded as were left alive gazed fearfully at the stern-faced, silent man riding on a white charger. His face meant

* Gordon Brooke-Shepherd, *Between Two Flags*, London 1973.

187

nothing to them but his air of command and the deference with which he was treated must have suggested to them that he was the dreaded Kitchener. With a gesture the Sirdar ordered the standard to be pulled up and carried in triumph before him; it was a concession to vainglory which he was to regret before the day was over.

The day was cripplingly hot, with a temperature in the sun of between 165° and 180°; the pace was fast, and for the British troops in particular, carrying thirty to forty pounds of equipment and many of them fresh to the Sudan, the march was a gruelling one. Little Frank Scudamore of the *Daily News* gave lifts to several of the more exhausted Tommies and by the time that Omdurman was no more than a mile or two away he had two tired men hanging on to his leathers on either side and fifteen rifles across his knees. Kitchener would have liked to keep straight on and occupy the city but, with the bulk of the dervish armies streaming away towards the south, the greatest reason for urgency had disappeared. If there were going to be street fighting then it was better that the troops should be rested first. Regretfully he ordered that the army should halt on the banks of the Khor Shambat, the wide stream which drained the plain between Omdurman and the Jebel Surgham and debouched in the Nile about three quarters of a mile before the outer fringes of the city.

At the best of times the Khor Shambat was muddy and squalid, on September 2, 1898 it took on a peculiarly loathsome aspect and carried the rich stink of death. 'The colour of weak tea, with a lot of milk in it,' Lt McNeill of the Seaforths described it, 'in which floated dead camels, horses, donkeys and even a few Dervishes. But what nectar!' 'A thick yellow vat of cocoa,' thought Captain Ray. To the weary and dehydrated Highlanders no cool pellucid burn could have been half so enticing. They flung themselves into the water, plunged their heads beneath

*Kitchener leaving the battlefield with his own flag and the Khalifa's
black banner in the rear*

the scum, gulped down great mouthfuls. 'I can still see
the "Jocks" up to their middles in the water, with their
kilts floating out on the surface like ballet-girls' skirts.'
The dangers of dysentery or, still worse, enteric fever
were obvious and a zealous staff-officer posted up and
insisted that all water should be boiled before drinking.
'I will not pollute this otherwise chaste narrative,' wrote
the prudent McNeill, 'by repeating some of the remarks
which I overheard from the "high-up stuff" as well as
from the "other ranks".' The staff-officer retreated discomfited, though he could have had the grim satisfaction
of saying 'I told you so' at many sick beds over the next
few weeks.

Then, by some logistic miracle, the supply camels came
up and it was boiling hot bully beef and biscuits for every
man. The menu was not perhaps a sybarite's delight nor
wholly suitable for the climate but none of the soldiers had
eaten since before dawn, they had been on the move and
fighting from then until half past two, and they would
have greeted still less palatable fare with rapturous delight.

Tiredness rolled away, the horrors of the march were forgotten, and it only required the horse of the Warwick's Quarter Master to roll over in the middle of the Khor and thoroughly duck its master to send the morale of the men soaring to fresh heights. By 4 p.m. they were not merely ready, they were anxious to be on the move.

And so the army set out on the last phase of its grand advance. The cavalry and camel corps were despatched to ride around the outskirts of the town, round up the fugitives and, above all, prevent the escape of the Khalifa. The infantry moved directly towards the centre of Omdurman, guided by the map which Slatin had prepared for them; 'a marvellous effort of memory,' commented Wingate. 'As accurate as if it had been drawn on the spot.' Maxwell's Sudanese Brigade was given the honour of leading the advance, the XIVth Sudanese on the left. In front even of these rode the Sirdar with the band of the XIth Sudanese playing lustily behind him and the black flag of the Khalifa proudly carried at his side.

Now all march discipline seemed forgotten as it became a wild race for the town. The 10th Sudanese brigade, still euphoric from their triumph over the Sheikh el Din, caught up with their old allies the Lincolns about half a mile from the first houses. To Hodgson's delight their band struck up the regimental march, the *Lincolnshire Poachers*. 'And by jove there was a howl when the old tune started, and we got in step and tried to keep pace, but the Companies and Regiments in front blocked us. The Sudanese were going half as fast again and as they caught up each company, we howled and they howled and shook their rifles in the air; great excitement! About half an hour later they had been blocked and halted and we passed them, our drums playing – they gave us a captured standard to carry ahead; more howls!'

In other parts of the advance the rivalry was less amicable. The Grenadiers were rash enough to get ahead of

Kitchener's entry into Omdurman

another of the Sudanese battalions and were startled by a sudden burst of firing over their heads. 'Where the devil does that come from?' asked Bagot nervously. 'Oh, it's the Gyppies behind,' said another, more experienced officer with somewhat forced cheerfulness. 'They always do that if you get in front of them.' The Sirdar now decided that the fun had gone far enough and galloped up, prudently preceded by a bugler playing the Cease Fire.

It was the only prudence which he showed that day. At first it was the enthusiasm of his own men which made his position in the van so perilous. A group of dervishes ran towards him, evidently to surrender. At once a nearby company of Sudanese opened fire; their first volley hardly even disturbed the dervishes but came near to doing serious damage among the headquarters staff. Furious, Kitchener pushed on still further ahead of the main

The Heavy Camel Corps

advance. As the army began to thrust its way into the
maze of mean and tortuous streets Kitchener, a conspicuous target in his white uniform and on his white horse,
was literally in the lead, a group of apprehensive staff
officers jostling behind him, wondering what would
happen if they ran into opposition.

Behind him the army had finally settled down into some sort of order; by necessity rather than desire since by now they were filtering into the city itself and could no longer advance in line. 'We pushed our way through, the Guards leading,' wrote a'Court, 'our drums and fifes playing the *British Grenadiers* as though we were going down St James's Street. . . . The fine piece of audacity of marching gaily into a fortified town as if it belonged to us met with a deserved reward: the whole resistance collapsed. One of the Baggara rode solemnly on a donkey into the middle of the army, pulled a rifle from under his *jibbah*, dismounted and began to shoot. Paradise was not refused him.'

There were not many such martyrs. As the Sirdar led the march down the great avenue which pierced the suburbs of the city a delegation of old white-bearded men with a mob of squalling women and children behind them came out to meet him. Slatin Pasha was assured by his fellow staff officers that it must be a group of his fathers-in-law with his wives and children come to welcome papa home. Slatin was not amused. This was his moment of glory and no flippancy must be allowed to mar it. As the old men came closer he turned to Kitchener and whispered importantly that the most venerable was the Emir of the Suburbs, a civil officer of high standing. The emir stepped forward, kissed the Sirdar's hand and begged for mercy for the people of Omdurman. 'Certainly,' replied Kitchener in fluent Arabic, 'if you will throw down your arms and not molest us.' With relief the emir handed over the keys of the city – a surrender even more nominal than usual since no member of the expeditionary force was able to discover any lock into which they could conceivably have fitted – and made a signal to his followers. In an instant heads blossomed from every window and every wall and the population surged out into the streets to welcome their conquerors. Kitchener hopefully interpreted this delirium as proving the people's satisfaction at the defeat of the Khalifa. There may have been an element of this, for Abdullahi's rule had done little to further the happiness of his people, but what the citizens must above all have been feeling was relief at finding that they were not after all to be massacred.

Nevertheless, the transformation which now overcame the dervish population was striking and vociferous. Soldiers returning from the battlefield simply turned their jibbahs inside out, rushed out into the streets, salaamed and called 'Peace be with You!' to the passing troops. Within a couple of days more than 2000 of them had joined the victor's army and were being busily drilled by British sergeants and N.C.O.s on the parade ground outside the city. Smith-Dorrien observed a still more rapid change of colours. As the 13th Sudanese marched into the great arena 'some thirty dervishes with brass instruments and drums, possibly the Khalifa's own band, placed themselves at the head of the regiment and, playing most excellent Sudanese marches, insisted on leading them, until they were voted a nuisance as they drowned words of command, when they were suppressed.'

So here at last was the goal of their long travail, the fabled city of Omdurman. Some at least of the British troops were still dreaming of exotic splendour and glanced from side to side in the constant hope that great palaces or mysterious temples would burst upon their eyes. They saw nothing but the nondescript squalor of what must then have been Africa's largest slum. Omdurman had nothing remarkable about it except its size. It was almost two miles from the outskirts of the city to the wall around the inner citadel, yet in all that distance the soldiers saw no single building of dignity or distinction, only an endless series of mud huts, some larger, some smaller, all drably feature-less. Apart from the one broad avenue, driven ruthlessly through the suburbs to ease the passage of the Khalifa's armies, there was only a labyrinth of narrow lanes, each one apparently identical with any other, each one pock-marked with deep holes and strewn with the detritus of urban life: a heap of dung, a dead donkey, a dying man.

Once the first euphoria was over the people who lined the streets were silent, watchful, certainly showing no hostility but equally slow to shout or wave. Steevens noticed that there were three women to every man: 'black women from Equatoria and almost white women from Egypt, plum-skinned arabs and a strange yellow type with square, bony faces and tightly ringleted black hair: old women, girls, mothers with babies, women swathed in cotton and closely veiled, women almost naked.' When there was any yelling or excitement it was the women who provided it while the men stood with their backs to the wall watching sullenly. Marching down the main avenue with the Lincolnshires Hodgson contrasted their bearing with that of his own well-fed and lively Tommies. They 'seemed very stolid poor brutes,' he noted pityingly, 'they have had such a bad time lately they are indifferent and callous to everything.'

The British troops stared about them in wild surmise, convinced that every hut they saw which seemed even slightly more ambitious than the others must be the Khalifa's palace and every woman on a donkey his senior wife. Their vagueness about their adversaries was daunt-ing; as noticeable, indeed, as their lack of information about their allies. A small group of dervish prisoners was led past their ranks. ''Urry up, Bill, come along!' called one private from the Warwicks, 'They've cotched the bloody Khedive.'

Every few minutes a shot indicated that some dervish still felt the urge to resist, or more probably, that a Sudanese of the allied army could not resist the temptation to take a pot-shot at some real or imagined enemy.

Kitchener seems to have done all he could to prevent unnecessary slaughter. According to Adolf von Tiedemann, he rode into the narrow streets and courtyards, wholly indifferent to the risk that some hot-headed dervish would take the chance to avenge his compatriots, holding up his hand and calling out *'Amân!'* – 'Peace!'

Among the units which were jostling for the lead as the army reached the outskirts of the city were the 13th Sudanese battalion under the command of the impetuous Smith-Dorrien. The Grenadiers had got ahead when the advance began down the main avenue but Smith-Dorrien doubled his men down a side alley, threaded his way through the maze and somehow contrived to rejoin the march a hundred yards ahead of the outraged Guards. Having secured the prize position he made sure he kept it by giving the cryptic order: 'Front form companies and quarter column on the leading company.' This, in less military language, meant that the Sudanese advanced down the avenue in line abreast, effectively blocking the progress of any other unit with aspirations to overtake them.

Their enterprise was rewarded when they arrived first at the great stone wall which girdled the inner citadel. Within it lay the prison, the mosque, or, more correctly, praying square, the Mahdi's tomb, the armoury and treasury, the Khalifa's palace and, perhaps, the Khalifa himself. Fourteen feet high, four feet thick, it loomed massively above the advancing troops. Was the cream of the dervish armies still within, waiting to fight to death in defence of its most sacred shrine, or had they already fled, leaving the fortress deserted behind them? As if in answer to the query there came the melancholy groan of the ombeya. To those who knew, the sound gave them the information which they needed. The Khalifa had still not left, there would be another fight before victory would be wholly won.

The Sirdar had fallen a little way behind and so Maxwell,

the brigade commander, sent Lt Blakeney hurrying back to ask for instructions. They were brisk and predictable: the place was to be taken before sunset. By now scattered firing was coming from the summit of the wall. It might have been possible to scale and storm it but the task would have been an expensive one. In other parts of the wall breaches had been made by artillery fire but here the massive stone face was inviolate. Maxwell instructed Smith-Dorrien to follow the wall to the left, down to the river, and find some entry there. With Kitchener once more in the van the 13th Sudanese set off again, leaving two guns of the 32nd Field Battery in case the enemy showed any life on the city side. Within a few minutes they had reached the river and swung right.

The advance-guard now found itself on a strip of ground about twenty feet wide with the high wall on their right, the Nile on their left, and the forts which had been built to control the river obstructing their way every hundred yards or so ahead of them. The forts had been shattered by the fire of the gun-boats and the howitzers from across the river but enough of the walls remained to provide shelter for a determined foe. With each fort clearly occupied and sporadic firing coming as well from the main wall the advance looked like being uncomfortable and perhaps costly. Smith-Dorrien was determined not to let the pace slacken. He took his men at the double along the foot of the wall, rushing each fort before the startled defenders had time to do more than fire a few shots. Then they came to 'a deep and forbidding khor' flowing from under the walls and forty or fifty feet wide. It was the main drain of the city, a thick and treacly yellow, scum-spattered and with the occasional dead and decomposing animal floating on its turgid depths. It would have been a nightmare to ford in any circumstances, with a brisk fire coming from the fort the other side there were few whom it would not have deterred. Smith-Dorrien

Lieutenant-Colonel Maxwell leading his Brigade into Omdurman

did not give the 13th Sudanese a second to contemplate
the grisly prospect; it was into the greasy slime, wading
up to the waist at its centre and out the other side before
the startled dervishes had time even to throw down their
guns and run. More and more it was becoming clear that
the garrison of Omdurman was totally demoralised; no
real fight was going to be put up.

Shortly after fording the drain the advancing Sudanese
found a heavy gate in the wall to their right. Shells had
partly torn it down and blown holes in the wall and it was
the work of a few moments to complete the job and force
an entry. They found themselves looking into the Beit el
Mal; literally the Treasury, though it served as the public
granary. Mountains of dates, thirty feet high and half an
acre in extent, the harvest of six years, were rotting in
putrid squalor; thousands of matting sacks, stuffed with
gums and ostrich plumes, lay damp and ruined. It was a
vision of fantastic prodigality; the riches of this poor

country that could so ill afford them squandered uselessly because of the total inadequacy of the administration to cope with the tribute it collected. It is an ill wind that blows nobody any good. Within half an hour several thousand of the women and children of Omdurman had heard that the Beit el Mal was open and were pouring through the breach. There were stomachs full that night which had not been satisfied for many months.

For Smith-Dorrien the sight was a disappointment. He would not find his way to the Khalifa's palace by way of a granary. The 13th Sudanese recoiled to the river bank and resumed their advance. It was more than a quarter of a mile before they reached the next gate, more massive and far more lavishly ornamented than the first. This time there could be no doubt, they had reached the main gate of the citadel. The firing from inside came faster than before but Smith-Dorrien was not in the least discomfited. This gate too had been partly shattered by gunfire; rammed vigorously by a convenient log it quickly began to yield. The screech of splintering timbers, a crash of falling masonry, and the door was down. An avenue stretched ahead, at the end of it the Mahdi's tomb. Now the end of the expedition was indeed in sight.

CHAPTER XII

Flight of a Demi-God

BY now it was some four hours since the Khalifa had left
the battlefield. His first act had been to go to the Mahdi's
tomb and pray: to pray for guidance perhaps, for forgive-
ness perhaps; who can guess what thoughts were running
through the mind of this man who had seen all he had
lived for so irreparably destroyed? Then he disposed of
his family and personal effects; his wives were despatched
in convoys towards the south so as to leave the citadel clear
for the bloody battle which he was contemplating. Finally
he walked to the praying square and gave orders that the
drums and obeyas should be sounded and his warriors
summoned. Tranquilly he awaited the rallying of the
faithful. He might be destined to die but at least he would
die in glory, surrounded by his followers and the bodies
of the infidel dead.

It took him perhaps half an hour before he accepted that
there were no faithful, that his followers had deserted him.
Some slunk into the square, surveyed him with mingled
shame and dismay and crept back the way they had come.
Others, more courageous or less feeling, jeered at him;
asked him why he was not sitting on his *farwah*, the
prayer-rug on which Arab leaders traditionally take their
place when they have been dishonoured and are awaiting
death. Dismayed, he summoned his secretary, Abou el
Gassim, and consulted him about what he should do next.
Satirically, perhaps, Abou el Gassim suggested that he
should go on praying; victory, no doubt, would then
follow. The Khalifa was unimpressed. He told him to go
round the palace collecting the remaining members of
his household; the secretary subserviently departed but

200

did not come back. There was still a handful of loyal attendants and Abdullahi despatched two of them to see how close the enemy had now got to the inner citadel. It took less than ten minutes for them to find out and return to their master. They had met Smith-Dorrien's advance guard just before it reached the entry to the Beit el Mal. It was obvious that within the next few minutes the Turks would be moving on in the direction of the Mahdi's tomb and the Khalifa's palace.

Now was the moment of decision. Should he remain and die with a handful of his bodyguard in an ineffective skirmish, or flee and live to fight another day. The strictest code of Arab honour dictated that he should die but the Khalifa had not won and retained his position by over-punctilious observance of the traditional laws. His mind was quickly made up. A detachment of the bodyguard was told to hold the infidels at bay for a precious few moments while the Khalifa quickly changed his clothes and slipped out through the network of passages at the rear of the palace. At the moment the 13th Sudanese battered down the main gate and began to advance up the avenue towards the praying square, the Khalifa was already away, trotting through the suburbs with a handful of followers in pursuit of his fleeing armies.

Smith-Dorrien's men advanced up the avenue towards the Mahdi's tomb. At the far end the road narrowed, just in front of a gate which led into an inner compound. If a last stand was going to be made it would surely be here. Pritchard was with the Sirdar directly behind the leading company of the Sudanese. An ineffective volley spattered around them and two Baggara horsemen emerged from the shadows and stationed themselves at each side of the gateway. Cautiously a score of Sudanese infantry edged forward in a semi-circle towards them. Suddenly the two horsemen charged. It was suicidal, but the Sudanese were taken by surprise and the Baggara were upon them before they could open fire. 'The leading horseman speared a Sudanese with a great spear about fifteen inches broad; it took the top of the man's head off just like the top of an egg.' A corporal was killed and two other men seriously injured before the two Baggara fell, riddled by bullets and spitted by bayonets.

The incident had taken only two or three minutes, but they were valuable minutes for the Khalifa. As the 13th Sudanese rushed the doorway and debouched on to the praying square they saw a small group of cavalry disappearing at the other end. It was the tail end of the Khalifa's escort. Already Abdullahi himself was one with the tide of fugitives that were pouring through the southern suburbs of the city and out into the desert beyond. Mounted baggara and dervish infantry, tottering greybeards and callow youths, women carrying babies and camels, horses and donkeys laden with the scanty goods and chattels of an impoverished population: even if they had been there the cavalry could never have detected their prey amidst such a multitude. Beatty on the *Metemma*, who from his raised platform could see over the houses, was instructed to open fire on the refugees. He did so, but with little enthusiasm; surely the day's slaughter had already been enough? One street which led down to the river was cleared from time to time with a hail of Maxim bullets, but the refugees merely sought more devious inland routes. The tide swept on unabated, and with it the Khalifa was borne out of the city, further and further from the men who had come so far to destroy him.

The advance guard of the invaders, with Maxwell in the lead, pushed on into the open space between the Mahdi's tomb and the Khalifa's palace. For the heart of one of Africa's greatest cities it could hardly have seemed more pitifully ignoble. 'Tiny round straw *tukls*,' wrote Steevens, 'mats propped up a foot from the earth with crooked sticks, dome-topped mud kennels that a man could just crawl into, exaggerated birds' nests falling to pieces of stick and straw.' At first it seemed deserted; only the three mangy lions which the Khalifa kept chained to posts outside his door stirred angrily in the uneasy quiet. Then a man slunk from one of the huts and cautiously approached the conquerors. Seeing that he was not instantly shot down, another followed, and another. Soon there were several hundred of them, many of them still carrying arms, members of the Khalifa's bodyguard who had refused to rally to him in his hour of desperation and now were ready to come to terms with the conqueror.

But what the terms might be was still uncertain. For a few nervous minutes the Anglo-Egyptians were heavily outnumbered; two companies of the 13th Sudanese, Maxwell and his staff marooned in a sea of potentially dangerous dervishes. An Arab-speaking officer rode forward and called to them to throw down their arms. For a moment it seemed doubtful whether they would obey; the mob stirred sullenly, uncertain which way it should jump. Then a shot was fired, a figure darted round the corner and disappeared, a Sudanese soldier fell dead. The incident could have precipitated a massacre, instead it led at once to surrender. Afraid of retaliation for the shooting, a dervish hurriedly flung his Remington on to the ground. Another rifle clattered on top of it and soon a massive pile was heaped in the middle of the square. Maxwell had the prisoners formed up and marched away. Within forty-eight hours they would be re-armed and formally enlisted in the Khedive's Egyptian army.

For a quarter of an hour or so the 13th Sudanese waited beside the Mahdi's tomb until the Sirdar, who had dropped behind in the final stages of the advance, should arrive to give further orders. The tedium was only broken by the eruption of a flock of the Khalifa's chickens who scurried unwisely across the beaten earth. Few of them survived and the cooking pots of the Sudanese were noticeably enriched that night. Then the familiar white horse appeared at the gateway and the squawking of the few indignant fowls still left alive was suffered to die down of its own accord. The Sirdar rode slowly into the centre of the enclosure, his staff behind him, the great black banner of the Khalifa still floating triumphant above his head. This last grandiloquent flourish was to cost the victors dear. One of the instructions given to the 32nd Battery of artillery when they were left outside the walls had been that they should open fire if they caught any glimpse of the Khalifa. The sight of his personal standard rearing proudly within a few yards of the Mahdi's tomb was taken as proof positive of his presence. A shell was immediately fired which screamed a few feet over the Sirdar's head and burst among a group of Sudanese, killing or wounding several of them.

For a moment everyone stood stupefied, unable to understand who could be firing at them. Then another shell burst a few yards from the first and a third followed. General Hunter dismounted, picked up a fragment and, in his most languid voice, remarked: 'Beg pardon sir, but these are our own shells.' Kitchener pondered an instant. 'Well, gentlemen, I don't see how we can stop it, and it would be a pity to lose our ticket when the day is won. I am afraid we must give them the honour.' He rode towards the gateway, his officers following with more haste than dignity. Almost all of them were clear when a fourth and final shell burst in the enclosure. A shard of shrapnel took away the ear from the pony of the *Daily News* correspondent, Frank Scudamore, while another killed instantly Hubert Howard of *The Times*.

Howard was one of those people who find irresistible the lure of adventure. All his life he had sought it, indifferent to his own fortune or safety. Earlier that day he had ridden with the Lancers and, for pure love of action, had taken part in the famous charge. He had survived unscathed. Now he perished in a foolish accident. In his obituary *The Times* applied to him the lines which Byron had written about his ancestor who had been killed in the charge of the 10th Hussars at Waterloo:

> '. . . *and when showered*
> *The death-bolts deadliest the thinnèd files along,*
> *Even where the thickest of war's tempest lowered,*
> *They reached no nobler breast than thine, young, gallant*
> *Howard.*'

As a trumpeter played the Cease Fire from a roof-top near the Mahdi's tomb in a belated effort to appease the fury of the 32nd Battery, Kitchener rode on towards the Khalifa's prison. Churchill, no doubt with some image of medieval dungeons in his mind, described it as a 'foul and gloomy den' but in fact, though foul enough, gloom in the literal sense was a commodity of which the prisoners would have liked rather more. The most unpleasant feature in a thoroughly disagreeable setting was the lack of any adequate shade. The gaol consisted of a series of ramshackle lean-tos set against a mud wall; a wall which would have done little to prevent an escape but was never put to the test since the prisoners were shackled with heavy irons which allowed only the most limited and painful movement. Above them loomed the gallows; tree trunks driven into the earth with a rough cross-piece stretched about ten feet above the ground. A body still dangled from one of them and their almost daily use had been a consistent deterrent for any prisoner contemplating defiance or a break for freedom.

Kitchener knew that the German merchant, Charles Neufeld, had been held at Omdurman for over eleven years but whether he was still alive and who else was incarcerated with him, was something which would only now be discovered. It seemed painfully possible that the

Neufeld with his native wife and children

Khalifa's parting act of vengeance might have been to massacre his prisoners. According to Idris, the chief gaoler, such orders had in fact been given. However, through humanity – as he assured the liberators – or through self-interest – as his former prisoners deemed more probable – he delayed the moment of execution on one pretext or another until the infidels were already at the gate. Then he concluded that it was too late to do anything so certain to enrage his future masters. He rushed to the place where Neufeld lay. The German was still burdened by three sets of leg irons, one weighing more than fourteen pounds, but the knowledge that rescue was on the way had raised his spirits to the point of hysteria. 'The place is filled with your English brothers,' Idris cried. A big, tall man had been asking particularly for him.

Helped by two of his gaolers and weeping so that he could hardly see, Neufeld stumbled towards the gate. Out of the mist before him he heard a hoarse voice demanding: 'Are you Neufeld? Are you well?' Kitchener stepped forward and gave his hand a hearty shake. 'Thirteen years we have been longing and waiting for this day,' stammered Neufeld, though his words can hardly have been audible, so deep was his emotion. The Sirdar glanced down

Neufeld in his German attaché's clothes

at the iron shackles. 'Can these be taken off now? I am going on.' Then, with a friendly slap on the shoulder, 'Neufeld, out you go!' Behind the dazed and almost speechless German clustered a group of the other European prisoners who had shared his misery: Sister Teresa Grigolini, the Mother Superior, who had been seized with Father Ohrwalder seven years before; Joseph Regnotti; a score or so of Greek traders. All were haggard and emaciated, though none was so heavily chained as Neufeld who had recently been suspected of plotting to escape.

Kitchener left behind a staff officer with instructions that he should do all that he could to make the prisoners comfortable. Neufeld's most urgent need was obviously to be freed from the monstrous weight of iron clamped around his legs. But this did not prove easy and, without the help of a vice and cold-chisel, it proved impossible to do more than loosen the more oppressive of his fetters. Eventually he was mounted on a horse and 'like a man drunk with new wine' was led off to the headquarters mess just north of the city. There he shared the celebration dinner of biscuits and water with a few scraps of his own prison bread to add variety to the military menu. But though the massive iron bar which weighed him down was removed by the farrier of the Warwickshires it was not till the next day, aboard the gun-boat *Sheikh*, that it proved possible to remove the leg irons and fully restore his long-lost liberty.

Meanwhile, Slatin, Maxwell and a group of Sudanese infantry moved on into the Khalifa's palace. Through the courtyard and into the building they rushed; into the Khalifa's favourite reception room, the walls entirely covered by large looking-glasses now smashed by shells or rioters; into the tawdry splendours of the bathroom, through the bedrooms and the unimpressive dining hall into the range of tiny chambers which made up the harem. All stood empty. By now the Khalifa was already in the desert, well on the way to a pre-arranged rendezvous where a group of camels were awaiting him.

For Slatin it was a bitter blow. Professionally it had above all been his job to ensure that Abdullahi did not escape; personally his longing for revenge possessed him. He galloped from the palace courtyard, almost beside himself with frustration. Lt Jeffreys was marching his platoon of the Grenadiers up the avenue when Slatin went by, his face distraught, lashing on his horse. 'I've missed him! By God, I've missed him!' he cried over his shoulder.

The pursuit and capture of the Khalifa now became the main preoccupation of the Anglo-Egyptian army. The 21st Lancers should have headed the chase but they were so battered after their ill-judged charge of the morning that the Sirdar ruled out their participation. It was left to Broadwood and the ever-willing Egyptian cavalry to take on the task. Haig had been with his men near the Khor Shambat since about 3 p.m., 'all worn out' he wrote. When they were ordered to move on round the perimeter of the city towards the western gate they assumed that it was so as to make camp and did not even bother to refill their water-bottles before setting off. At the gate, however, they saw Slatin galloping towards them 'full of excitement', bearing instructions to set off at once after the Khalifa. 'I won't tire you with an account of our sufferings during this pursuit,' wrote Haig to Sir Evelyn Wood, proceeding to do so, 'sufferings which half-an-hour's forethought and preparation would have prevented.' Some small part of the forethought, it is fair to say, might have been his own.

However meticulous the preparations, it would have been a rugged ride. Slatin brought his unwelcome news at 7 p.m. Within ten minutes Broadwood had procured a couple of Kababish guides who knew the country to the south. No extra supplies were carried because it was intended to despatch the *Metemma* up-river later the same night with forage for the horses and provisions for the men. A rendezvous was hurriedly fixed for a point on the Nile above Omdurman and the exhausted cavalry set off once more.

The project was doomed to failure from the start. For one thing, nobody had any idea in which direction the Khalifa had gone. Few haystacks could be larger than the Sudan, few needles smaller than a little group of travellers. Everyone whom Slatin or Broadwood questioned gave a different answer; sometimes, no doubt, out of ignorance, more often from loyalty towards their defeated ruler. To avoid the main flow of retreating dervishes the cavalry struck inland. Then the column ran into swampy ground. Hours were lost as the horses floundered in the wet sand; then, the marsh once behind them, they found themselves in harsh, rocky country where the least slip could break a limb. At 11 p.m. Broadwood decided it would be folly to continue until the moon rose. This it did at 3 a.m. and the weary cavalry, cramped and aching after their uncomfortable rest, with only a handful of biscuit and a few gulps of stagnant water to sustain them, were after their wild goose again. At 7 a.m. they neared the river and saw the outline of the *Metemma*. 'Our spirits soared,' wrote an officer with the expedition, 'at the thought of a square meal and, better still, a long, hot drink.'

The rejoicing was quickly cut off. When the cavalry reached the bank they saw that the gun-boat was more than 400 yards away; between them an interwoven mass of reeds and rotting tree trunks put any sort of physical contact out of the question. Impotent, the hungry cavalry men stood on the bank and watched their breakfast linger out of range and then steam farther up the river. It was agreed that gun-boat and cavalry should proceed together towards the south in the hope of finding a point where the bank was more readily accessible.

It was a hopeless quest. The bank got more rather than less marshy, the cavalry were forced farther and farther into the desert. The day was not wholly without its compensations, however. The camel corps, toiling gallantly along in the rear, were told that a group of dervishes of great importance was hiding in some bushes a little distance off. Exultantly they swooped. It was not the chief prize but instead a group of the Khalifa's wives, including the gross Fatima, senior wife and mother of Sheikh el Din. Green-Wilkinson of the Rifle Brigade surveyed the captives critically. 'One was a very pretty girl of about 17, half Circassian, half Shazieh, the only decent-looking woman I have seen in the Sudan. They were all very friendly, but hungry, and were sent back to the Sirdar.' It is unlikely the Sirdar was particularly gratified by the gift, even by the Circassian seventeen-year-old, but the capture of Fatima in particular caused a sensation in Omdurman and completed the demoralisation of the Khalifa and his followers.

Broadwood decided that this would have to do. By 2 p.m. they had only been able to advance another seven miles, the biscuit was exhausted, there was only one small meal left for the horses and the *Metemma* was farther out of range than ever. No more could be asked of man or beast. Slatin was for pushing on still further, but Slatin was notoriously unbalanced on this subject. 'Old Rowdy was most useful and behaved well throughout,' was Wingate's comment, but Wingate had not had to endure Slatin's importunities through the rigours of the pursuit. Broadwood firmly over-ruled the vengeful Austrian. Even as it was he had almost left the decision too late. It was not until 11 a.m. on the following day that the cavalry trickled back into Omdurman and the condition of both men and horses made it perfectly clear that the Khalifa had come close to gaining a swift, if unmerited revenge.

Meanwhile, back at the city, the night of September 2 had offered little in the way of sleep for the triumphant victors. Orders had been given that the bulk of the army should bivouac on the western fringes of the city; but this seemingly simple task proved hard to carry out. Night was falling, the only land mark was the Mahdi's tomb, the population seemed to derive a little belated satisfaction from mis-directing the troops. Sweating and cursing, almost dropping with fatigue, the army and its transport surged through the maze of narrow streets. Here and there a dervish decided that enough had not yet been done to save the national honour and fired from some dark corner at the passing soldiers, but such incidents were rare. A sullen hostility was usually the worst that the conquerors were called on to endure.

The Sirdar himself did not come together with the rest of his headquarters staff and the baggage until two hours after nightfall. They bedded down, as they later discovered, on the site of the Khalifa's old execution ground. Rawlinson stumbled around searching for lights so that Kitchener could dictate a despatch. The camel carrying the lamps seemed to have gone astray. Frank Scudamore of the *Daily News* produced some large wax matches. Kitchener squatted on his haunches while Wingate lay on his stomach scribbling down the Sirdar's words and Rawlinson and another staff officer knelt on either side. The uncertain, flickering lights, the crouching figures, provided a strangely chiaroscuro effect, like some old illustration of villains plotting in a sinister underworld.

The background to the Sirdar's labours was still more macabre. The army had by now fanned out over a wide area, outside the city proper and yet still in a densely populated area. A few days before the Khalifa, in an effort to check a mass exodus from the city at the news of the approaching enemy, had ordered that all beasts of burden not needed by the army should be slaughtered. There had been much evasion of his decree, but the massacre had still been on a massive scale, as the Rifle Brigade had cause to know. They found themselves camped in a graveyard, strewn with 'dead donkeys, camels, horses and a good many other things. . . . The stench was enough to kill any human being,' noted Corporal Emery philosophically, 'but we had to put up with it till morning.' Other regiments were a little more fortunate but none were comfortable and few found their camping-sites substantially more salubrious. Beyond their outposts, from the desert, came the whispers, the groans, the cries, of the thousands of dervishes, most of them wounded, who were creeping discomfited from the battlefield. Their one preoccupation was to get away; to where they did not know but away, away from the terrible rifle volleys, the bursting shrapnel, the charging Lancers. Many of them would survive, some survive to fight again, but few that night had thoughts beyond the horizon and the greatest distance that they could put between themselves and the Sirdar's armies.

Things were no more tranquil within the city itself. Many of the Sudanese troops had at one time fought with the Khalifa, several hundred of them had been recruited since the battle of the Atbara. No man hates his former comrades as full-bloodedly as a turncoat and these men had scores to settle.

Ibrahim el Yakbabi heard his name being called from the door of his house. He peered out and saw a former slave, now wearing the uniform of Kitchener's army. Thinking that this old friend had come to cheer him in the hour of defeat he greeted him affably and held out his hand. His answer was a bullet in the stomach. 'His family came out and found the soldier, who had been known to them since childhood, trampling with his boots on the stomach of the corpse; and all went in and hid themselves, fearing death.' Babikr Bedri, now safely back in Khartoum, saw a negro soldier leading a slave girl by the hand. The girl's former master ran up and tried to reclaim her. 'The soldier at once loaded his rifle and shot him, and he leapt up in the air and fell to the ground. Then the soldier took the girl's hand again; and they went away laughing loudly.' The two were brother and sister and both had been brought up in the house of the murdered man.

Egerton of the Camerons heard the distant firing and warned one of his sentries not to fire unless it was essential. 'Oh, no, Sir; a'wn thinkin' it's only the people rejoicin' at the victory!' was the optimistic answer. 'The noises, the screams of agony and terror, the shouting and the constant discharge of rifles and whistling of bullets – were somewhat disconcerting,' was Egerton's temperate summary of the situation.

In spite of it all, the army slept. Few of the men had blankets and the night was cold. In the distance the war-drums throbbed, summoning what was left of the faithful to re-form their ranks. Ghostly shapes loomed up out of the darkness, were challenged and vanished back into the night. None of it could disturb the troops. Though the discomfort remained, the danger was past, the victory was won. Now at last they could relax and look to their future. The relief was great.

CHAPTER XIII

'Surely now he is Avenged'

SEPTEMBER 3 dawned with the slight chill which presaged another scorching day to come. The army stirred early; even if the conditions had been more congenial there could be no long lie that day. Stragglers had to be rounded up and regiments re-formed; supplies assembled and distributed; equipment checked; the dervish prisoners dealt with and the city secured. All the stocktaking and re-organisation which follows a great victory lay ahead – it would be time enough to rest when the army had travelled back down the river and Omdurman become but a distant memory.

The first duty was to the allied wounded. Among the British troops who had survived from the battle of the Atbara, gloom about the medical organisation could hardly have been deeper. 'The doctors with the English brigade were r—— and all the arrangements worse,' wrote Felix Ready indignantly about the earlier battle. 'I really could write about the horrors of these, and might, and fill pages.' Since then there had been improvement. Considerable reinforcements had arrived and Colonel Sloggett of the Medical Corps, with brisk efficiency and humanity, had brought some sort of order into the ramshackle service. But now Sloggett himself lay severely wounded with a bullet through his lungs, shot while tending the wounded during the attack on Macdonald's brigade. Worse still, the three barges which had been equipped to act as floating hospitals had abruptly been ordered away from the battlefield in case they impeded the operations of the gun-boats. When the general advance from El Egeiga began the wounded had to be hurriedly loaded on to a nearby ammunition barge. After they had been joined by the casualties from the 21st Lancers the congestion became appalling: dead and dying huddled together in a temperature of 119° in the shade with empty boxes serving as an operating table and the chloroform blown away in the occasional gusts of torrid wind. Eventually the barge was towed upstream by a passing steamer and deposited beneath the walls of Omdurman. It was not till the following day that hospital barges and casualties were at last united.

But the British victims fared better than their native allies. The Egyptian and Sudanese troops had to rely on a tiny body of ill-trained Egyptian surgeons and orderlies. In theory their expatriate colleagues were also subject to the same ministrations but, as the *British Medical Journal* lucidly expressed it, 'British officers in the Egyptian army naturally do not care about being treated by them for a serious injury.' While Egyptian wounded were stacked along the bank, the British members of the Khedive's army joined their compatriots on the crowded barge.

None of the casualties, white or coloured, can have passed a comfortable night. Even with the slight casualties born by the Anglo-Egyptian army basic essentials like bandages and disinfectant were in short supply. Bagot of the Grenadiers, himself a casualty, asked a fellow victim what would have happened if the troops had had to fight their way house-by-house through the city of Omdurman and the streets had been strewn with allied casualties. 'What happened at the Atbara,' was the chilling reply. 'They would have been left to die.' Churchill visited the sick and was characteristically unable to control his indignation. 'My remarks on the treatment of the wounded – again disgraceful – were repeated to (Kitchener) and generally things have been a little unpleasant,' he noted, with what sounds like satisfaction. 434 wounded: 153

British, 281 Egyptian and Sudanese, had cause to share his judgment.

Three British and two native officers had died while for the other ranks the corresponding figures were twenty-five and eighteen. A few of the bodies were not recovered; the remainder were buried on the banks of the Nile. The burial ground was placed on a small knoll looking over the river towards Khartoum. In the distance could be seen a clump of green trees concealing the gutted ruin in which Gordon had perished fourteen years before. So the men who had fought so hard and marched so far to avenge the general were never to reach their ultimate goal yet at least found their final resting place within view of their destination.

Some fifty lives cut short, fifty families deprived – grim enough, yet a trifling cost for a major victory. Cholera, enteric fever and other diseases were to carry off many more before the soldiers saw their homes again. The death toll seems almost derisory when contrasted with the massacre among the dervish army. Nobody counted the enemy dead; nobody knew how many crawled from the battlefield to die in crevices among the rocks or to be carried away by the waters of the Nile. Many people hazarded guesses, all with some shadow of verisimilitude. From the sum of their computations one may estimate that a little under ten thousand of the Khalifa's army perished on the day of battle. There were at least as many wounded, probably nearer twenty thousand, and of these a quarter, on the most conservative estimate, can hardly have survived for more than two or three more days. Five thousand prisoners were taken; the number could have been three times as great if the cavalry had had the energy or inclination to round them up. The dervish army was shattered, never to re-assemble.

The battlefield was repulsive to eye, ear and above all, nose. Over an area of several hundred acres the dead were strewn; the bloated, contorted corpses heaped thick around the fallen standards of their emirs. Where the black flag of the Khalifa had been captured, a mound of bodies, three deep in places, showed where the cream of the dervish army had perished in defence of their leader's honour.

But it was not the dead so much as the dying who filled the sight-seeing British troops with pity and horror. The stump of a man, with hardly a bone unbroken, somehow clinging on to life and consciousness; another, with both knee-caps smashed, who had crawled more than 800 yards towards the river yet still had nearly two miles to go before he would reach the life-giving water. That he was doomed, that almost all his fellow-victims were doomed, was grimly obvious to the observers. They did what little they could to help – a gulp of water here, a wound bound up there – but the catastrophe which had overtaken the dervishes was too great for any such palliative. On September 4, when things were better organised, the English division sent out about 150 mules, each carrying six water-bottles and some biscuit, but even this made little difference. The resources to succour the injured did not exist, even if the will had been far stronger. So they were left to die, clinging obstinately to the last flicker of life in their hideously crippled bodies until the merciless – or perhaps merciful – sun completed what the bullets and the shrapnel had begun.

The prisoners were probably the most fortunate of all the dervish army. Kitchener wrote petulantly to Cromer that he had 30,000 cooks and concubines on his hands and had no use for them in either capacity. It seemed indeed as if half the population of Omdurman was anxious to serve the conqueror. The Sirdar shooed them away from his camp but still they came back, begging for food, for jobs, for news of their relatives. The prisoners of the battlefield, however, were a different matter. Except for a hard core who refused to serve the infidel they allowed themselves

Gordon Memorial Service, Khartoum, 1898
Painting by R. Caton Woodville

to be recruited *en bloc* into the army of the Khedive. Two days drilling, a token change in uniform, and the transformation was complete. The men who had flung themselves so gallantly against the zariba at El Egeiga now found themselves aligned with the men who had so recently shot them down. It was perhaps fortunate that their new-found loyalty was not to be subjected to the test of battle.

For the less ambitious sight-seer the centre of attention was the Mahdi's tomb. A huge hole had been blasted in the egg-shaped dome and rubble strewed the two great blocks of stone which covered the body. Within, the interior was rapidly being stripped of its sparse furnishings. The brass railings around the romb and the black and red cloth covering to the catafalque had already vanished and the yellow-lettered panels with texts from the Koran were eagerly carried off by souvenir hunters. Soon nothing remained but the stark grave itself.

But this degradation was not enough to satisfy the Sirdar. Advised by Slatin he concluded that the tomb, already regarded with veneration by the dervishes, would become the rallying point of a revolutionary movement and help the Khalifa reinstate himself as a threat to the Anglo-Egyptian conquerors. The tomb must be razed to the ground and the Mahdi's body flung into the Nile. Though Churchill denounced this act as 'wicked' and liberal opinion was predictably outraged, Kitchener's decision could probably be justified on political grounds. Certainly the apparition of the Mahdi's inadequately embalmed and decomposing body was a sad blow to those of his followers who believed that he had merely gone on a visit to heaven and would soon return to resurrect his earthly body. But it was still a distasteful operation and did little to enhance Kitchener's reputation for chivalry. 'The bones of the Mahdi have been chucked into the river, which I think rather bad form . . .' was Captain Sparks's comment and as a judgment it does not seem too intemperate.

The demolition of the tomb itself was entrusted to Monkey Gordon; thus adding a still stronger flavour of personal vengeance to what should have been an operation of clinical dispassion. A few charges of gun-cotton and a working-party of Sudanese quickly ended the existence of this monument; trivial in architectural significance, vast in the role which it had played in the minds and hearts of the people of the Sudan. Now it is reconstructed, yet the old magic has never been recaptured.

The Mahdi's 'unusually large and shapely' skull was put to one side when the rest of his corpse was disposed of in the Nile. Kitchener, almost incredibly, toyed with the idea of mounting it in silver to serve as an inkwell or a drinking cup. Hurriedly he abandoned the idea when he realised the revulsion that it would cause in Britain and instead announced his intention of presenting the skull to the College of Surgeons where he had a hazy impression Napoleon's intestines were similarly preserved. Captain Sparks would no doubt have felt this a still more egregious piece of bad form and Queen Victoria, as so often, shared the instincts of her subjects. She expressed her displeasure firmly and Lord Salisbury telegraphed to Cromer that this nonsense must be put a stop to. 'I am very sorry that Her Majesty should consider that the Mahdi's remains were unjustifiably treated,' wrote Kitchener to Cromer in some dismay. 'I will have the skull buried as the Queen desires.' In the end it found a dignified if unpretentious resting place in the Muslim cemetery at Wadi Halfa.

After the tomb the Arsenal was the favourite resort of the sight-seer and souvenir hunter, so much so, indeed, that a prize committee was appointed to take charge of the contents and decide how they should be distributed. Egerton of the Seaforths was a member and was amazed by the magpie splendours he found within. Gatlings and Nordenfeldt guns and Remington rifles which would have proved invaluable on the battlefield were heaped carelessly in great piles beside chain mail which had survived from the Crusades and spears captured from the Abyssinian infantry a few years before. The most recent addition was a cavalry officer's sword, its scabbard vanished, which had been lost in the Lancer charge and brought in as a solitary trophy of victory an hour or two later.

But the arms were the least extraordinary part of this strange collection. Among the treasures of which Egerton had charge were: 'a large regal-looking ceremonial staff with the Lion of Abyssinia carved on its head'; General Gordon's telescope; a pot of sardines wrapped up in a sheet of the *Étoile Belge* of March 24, 1894; a pair of field glasses which Lt Charles Grenfell had lost at El Teb in 1883; some hippopotamus hides; and a curious belt set with spikes protruding inwards, the use of which was obscure but can only have been unpleasant. The more interesting objects were set aside for museums, royalty and the Sirdar's private gratification; the rest were auctioned in aid of military charities.

But without recourse to auctions most of the more enterprising officers did pretty well for themselves. Felix Ready was particularly successful. 'I have a fine collection of plunder,' he boasted, 'but have to keep it very dark. My cheek, I think, is extraordinary as I have actually got one of the two marble slabs with inscriptions in Arabic from off the Mahdi's tomb.' As if this was not enough he had one of Neufeld's iron anklets, 'two drums, spears, a steel helmet, guns, swords, flags, everything in fact'. Not quite everything. One of Smith-Dorrien's men looted a very fine and tame Crowned Crane from the Mahdi's house. It was taken to Malta and thence, by means of H.M.S. *Dido*, to the Scilly Isles where it lived for six years and survives stuffed in Tresco Abbey to the present day.

There was little else with which the victorious army could divert itself. Captain Sparks strolled round part of the city with a group of friends. 'An enormous collection of wretched mud brick hovels,' he described it. 'It seems a sin to have wasted blood and treasure and immense hard labour over the likes of it.' His judgment would probably have been echoed by nine out of ten men in Kitchener's army.

One last duty remained before the expeditionary force could deem its task fully completed. The ghost of Gordon still stirred abroad and must be fully laid. The degree to which his memory possessed the British leaders is well shown by the Sirdar's General Order issued the day after the battle which congratulated the troops on their excellent behaviour 'resulting in the total defeat of the Khalifa's forces and worthily avenging Gordon'. Now Kitchener announced what was to be the crowning point of the expedition; a parade and memorial service in honour of the murdered general outside the walls of his former palace.

There were unexpected problems before the service could take place. Four chaplains had accompanied the army – Anglican, Methodist, Presbyterian and Roman Catholic – and it was Kitchener's intention that each of them should play some part in the service. This premature oecumenism did not at all appeal to the Rev. Mr Watson, the Anglican padre, who categorically refused to take part in any such circus. General Wauchope, himself a Presbyterian, failed to persuade him and returned for help to Kitchener. The Sirdar received the news with ominous calm and sent for Monkey Gordon. 'What religion was your uncle?' he enquired. Gordon replied that he was Church of England 'but that he was a man who would say his prayers equally well in a Roman Catholic church'. Satisfied, Kitchener informed Mr Watson that his presence was no longer required with the army and he should return at once to Cairo. Watson rapidly concluded that strict orthodoxy was, after all, perhaps not quite so important. He himself hurried to headquarters and made his peace with the angry Sirdar. 'What broad-minded men some of our clergy are, so charitable!' was Bagot's characteristically splenetic comment.

On Sunday September 4 the gun-boats *Abu Klea* and *Melik* brought representatives of every regiment and corps across the Nile to Khartoum. The stone quay along the river-front was crumbling and dilapidated, beyond it a huge accacia tree had run riot and obscured much of the palace. Only the wreck remained of the building Gordon knew. The upper storey had collapsed, the windows were blocked with bricks, the staircase from which he had confronted his assailants was now a heap of rubble. The lush undergrowth had spread over what once had been stables and outhouses so that only the stone and stucco of the main façade could still be discerned for what it was. Compared with Omdurman, wrote Bennet Burleigh, Khartoum 'wore an air of romance and loveliness'; the words were strong ones but there was a haunted beauty about the ruins which struck the hardened fighting men of Kitchener's army with a kind of awe.

The troops were formed up in front of the palace in three sides of a rectangle; the Egyptians to the left as they faced the river, the British to the right. On the roof of the palace, within a few feet of the spot where Gordon had died, two tall flag posts had been erected. By one stood Lt Stavely of the Royal Navy and Captain Watson of the King's Royal Rifles; by the other Bimbashi Mitford and the Sirdar's Egyptian A.D.C. The Sirdar raised his hand; the Union Jack flew out from the first of the flag posts; a $12\frac{1}{2}$-pounder aboard the *Melik* fired once; the band played *God Save the Queen*. Another signal, another shot, the Khedivial tune and the Egyptian flag was flying

224

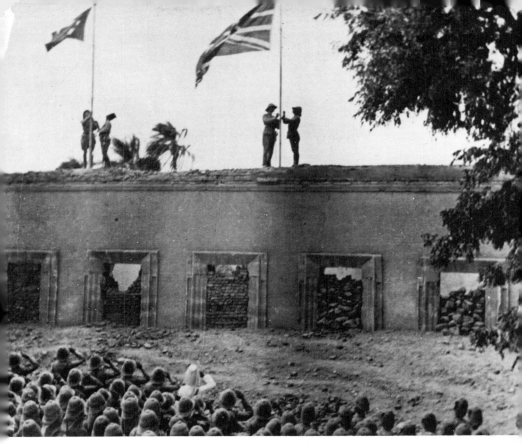

Flags are raised in Omdurman

from the other post. It took a cynic like Bagot to point out that the British flag was some four times the size of its Egyptian counterpart.

Three cheers were ordered for the Queen and given lustily; three cheers for the Khedive, and they came with a reasonable appearance of enthusiasm. Then the *Melik* fired a twenty-one-gun salute. No blank was available so live shot was fired over the heads of the congregation into the one-must-hope deserted plains beyond the city. 'The moan of the shells hurtling through the still air added a weird and unusual note to the ceremony,' noted Rawlinson. The reverberations of the last shot died away and Wauchope stepped forward. 'Three cheers for the Sirdar,' he called. The roar that followed far surpassed the efforts for Queen and Khedive. The cheering was 'by order' commented Bagot sourly but at that moment it is doubtful if many soldiers felt anything but real enthusiasm for their commander.

And so, with the Guards' band playing the *Dead March* from *Saul* and the Sudanese the march from Handel's *Scipio*, began the service proper. The Presbyterian minister read the 15th Psalm, the Anglican led the congregation in the Lord's Prayer. Then the pipers, accompanied by muffled drums, played the *Coronach* as a lament. About a hundred of the local inhabitants had clustered at the far end of what had once been the lawn. Most of them had known Gordon, several had served him in posts around the palace. As the pipers took up the dirge they broke into a shrill, wailing cry and the twin laments, so different and yet so curiously similar, blended in a tortured harmony which Gordon, if he had heard it, would surely have approved. And now it was the time for *Abide With Me* – Gordon's favourite hymn, or so, at least, it was generally agreed. It was to the band of the XIth Sudanese that fell the honour of playing the tune and there can have been hardly a man in the British contingent at least who did not know the words:

> '*Where is death's sting? Where Grave, thy victory? . . .*
> *I triumph still if Thou abide with me.*'

As the threne wore mercilessly towards its melancholy end, the sense of comradeship, the pain at friends departed; the glory of an object accomplished, a holy grail attained; above all a memory of that intolerable, indomitable little man who had died here so many years before, welled up in the hearts of the participants.

> '*Heaven's morning breaks, and earth's vain shadows flee;*
> *In life, in death, O Lord, abide with me.*'

Count von Tiedemann. the German military attaché, in

his magnificent white uniform of the Cuirassiers, blew his nose with a formidable trumpet-blast. To his neighbour, in a guttural whisper, he muttered that he wished he was an Englishman. 'He might well have wished it at that particular moment at any rate,' commented Captain Sparks.

The wail died away on the slight breeze which fanned the island. Father Brindle, the Roman Catholic padre whose gentleness, generosity and joy in life had made him the best-loved man in the army, stepped forward to give the benediction. 'I have never, except in family trouble, felt so like bursting into tears,' recorded the normally unimpressionable Rawlinson. 'The Sirdar had great round tears on his cheeks.' He turned to Hunter and asked him to dismiss the parade on his behalf.

Kitchener's impassivity had for once cracked. After the service, noted a'Court, he was very much changed: 'the sternness and the harshness had dropped from him for the moment, and he was gentle as a woman. . . . The lines of thought had gone out of his face. His manner had become easy and unconstrained. He was very happy.' After the parade had been dismissed and the senior officers had each in turn come up to shake him by the hand, he walked in the desolation which had once been Gordon's garden, speaking of the man whom he had come so far to avenge with admiration, even love. It was one of the few occasions in his life when he was heard to speak with gratitude of those who had worked with and for him.

Major Snow, now Brigade Major of Macdonald's brigade, had been with the Camel Corps on the ill-fated expedition to rescue Gordon. On that occasion he had carried with him a half-bottle of champagne which he had boasted would be drunk the day Khartoum was relieved. The bottle had remained unbroached and, by some miracle, unbroken. Now Snow was at last on the spot which he had expected to reach so long before.

Ceremoniously the bottle was opened and passed around a little group of veterans of the two campaigns. The champagne was far from cool and one may doubt whether it had been improved by its long peregrinations, but few half-bottles can have given greater pleasure to the drinkers.

The soldiers now rambled over the ruins of the palace and the garden, half in pilgrimage, half in hunt for souvenirs. Gordon's head gardener had remained on the premises all the intervening years, doing what little he could to maintain some sort of order in the encroaching jungle. He was congratulated and solemnly re-instated. The pomegranates and the passion flowers were in wild bloom; the orange trees, the date-palms and the grape-vines had grown almost unchecked in a luxurious frenzy. 'It must have been a paradise at one time,' wrote Hodgson. 'Now it is all a tangle. I cut a swagger stick, but I fear I have lost it.' All around him officers and men were pulling off leaves, flowers or green oranges to carry home as tokens of the fact that they had reached their goal. There were some unsuspected hazards for the sightseers. Wandering around the ruins, Lt Percival of the Fighting Fifth lit a cigarette and dropped the match to the ground. Never has litter-lout been more abruptly punished. The spot he had chosen had been used as a powder magazine and the blast threw the unfortunate subaltern twelve feet away. Though his eyes were shielded by his cumbersome helmet, he ended up with severe burns on the face and arms; a minor blemish on a day of otherwise unlimited rejoicing.

And so the troops mustered once more in front of the palace; relaxed, cheerful, yet sobered by their brush with the ghosts of the past. It was not a spectacle which would have graced the parade grounds of Europe. Major Bagot noted with mingled admiration and dismay, 'the troops that had completed their long and arduous task standing there in their shabby, worn clothes, perhaps realising for the first time what the task was and what had been accomplished.' It was indeed a moment of fulfilment. Of such a moment it would be pleasant to record that only the most elevating, the most Christian sentiments filled the minds of the victors. Instead it was fierce satisfaction at vengeance wreaked which bulked largest in the soldiers' minds. 'Gordon avenged after more than thirteen years,' wrote Bagot exultantly and almost every record of the service at Khartoum implies in some way that now at last the ghost of the martyred general could rest in peace. Nor was it only the troops in the Sudan who felt this way. Kitchener wrote to the Queen, describing the service in terms so lyrical, so moving, that one suspects Lord Edward Cecil must have been called in to do the drafting. Victoria wept, yet swelled with pride. 'Surely, now he is avenged,' she noted in her diary.

It was the voice of her people. The paean of triumph which rose from every class and every part of Britain spoke above all of pride regained, of a stain on the nation's honour at last expunged. Every form of popular rejoicing – from the humblest bonfire in the country hamlet to the glittering Guildhall banquet – was fresh proof of the unanimity of the national mood. It was the last fine flourish of confident imperialism; free from nagging pangs of conscience or irritating doubts about the ethics of a colonial enterprise. Few stopped to ponder on the real worth of the achievement, to calculate the odds or to wonder whether the glory had not been too dearly bought. Self-glorification, rampant and unabashed, enjoyed what was to be almost its final fling. It is ironic to consider the distaste, even disgust, with which Gordon himself would have observed the exultation of his countrymen. It is doubtful whether any Victorian stopped to consider whether the man in whose name the expedition had originally been launched might not now be turning uneasily in his grave. Why should he, after all? Had he not been avenged?

The body of the Khalifa, November 1899

And so the troops sailed back to Omdurman to prepare
for the final exodus. The captains and the kings departed.
Kitchener proceeded up the Nile to Fashoda to check on
the activities of a certain Major Marchand who was
reported to be raising the flag of France in the heart of
what any reasonable man must concede to be a zone of
British interest. The bulk of his forces returned downstream
to Cairo and thence to Crete, Gibraltar or the British Isles.
Soon the army was dispersed, the Sirdar cast into a new
and yet more refulgent incarnation as Governor General
of the Sudan. Another few months passed and Wingate
caught up with the Khalifa, slew him, and thus put a

belated full-stop to the story which had begun in 1885. The soldiers departed, to be replaced by a new breed of proconsuls and civil servants: dedicated men prepared to sacrifice the delights of home so as to bring the benefits of British civilisation to even the most benighted of the heathen. They were good men on the whole, and they did a good job on the whole. Their time passed and in the end they too departed.

And after three quarters of a century, what remains? The sere rocks, the barren sands, the desolation. A Russian radar station crowns the peak of the Jebel Surgham; the battlefield is now a designated military area, inexorably barred to spies, trippers or inquisitive historians. Otherwise there is nothing that Kitchener would not have recognised, that Abdullahi would not immediately have identified as the scene of his humiliation. The dervish corpses rotted in the sun or were buried in graves hastily scratched a few inches below the surface. The jackals and the vultures ate their fill. The glory lingered when the odour of death had vanished but that too now has largely faded.

Omdurman today is hardly a place of pilgrimage. Who, indeed, would be the pilgrims? No one cherishes the memory of defeat, and the descendants of the victors prefer to take their packaged holidays in a milder climate and more seductive scenes. Time hath an art to make dust of all things, as much of a man's reputation as of his body, of the things that he did, of the reasons for which he did them. Who knows or cares today why some eighty thousand men fought to the death for the possession of this benighted stretch of sand? Was it the working out of Britain's imperial destiny; the defence of our dependant, Egypt; the clarion-call for vengeance? The rocks and the sand hold no answer. Perhaps there is no answer. Perhaps at this moment some Arab Kaspar squats beside the Nile

231

Chief tomb of the Dervishes at Kerreri

and contemplates the skull with which his grandchildren are playing:

> '*They say it was a shocking sight*
> *After the field was won;*
> *For many thousand bodies here*
> *Lay rotting in the sun;*
> *But things like that, you know, must be*
> *After a famous victory.*'

But what was it all about, asks little Abdullah; and what good did it do, asks Fatima, his sister?

> '*Why that I cannot tell,*' *said he,*
> *But t'was a famous victory.*'

Acknowledgements
Bibliography
List of Illustrations
Index

Acknowledgements

By gracious permission of Her Majesty The Queen I have been able to consult letters from Sir Reginald Wingate and Lord Kitchener in the Royal Archives.

I owe much gratitude both to those who have enabled me to study manuscript material in museums or private collections and to those who have eliminated some at least of the blunders caused by my limited knowledge of military matters. In particular I would like to mention The Marquess of Anglesey; Major Barker (Queen's Own Highlanders); Major Bartelot (Royal Artillery); Mr Gordon Brook-Shepherd; Sir Arthur Bryant; Mr N. Collett; Lt General Sir George Collingwood; Mr Leo Cooper; Mr Dineen of the R.U.S.I.; Her Majesty's Ambassador in Khartoum, Mr Gordon Etherington-Smith; Sir James Fergusson; Mr I. J. Foster, Keeper of Oriental Books at Durham University; Lt Colonel ffrench Blake (17/21st Lancers); Mr Alan Goulty; Major Jessup (Royal Anglian Regiment); Mr King of the War Office Library; Mr Boris Mollow of the National Army Museum; Lt Colonel Pratt (Royal Northumberland Fusiliers); Mrs J. H. Rose; Lt Colonel Ryan (Royal Warwickshire Regiment); Major T. P. Shaw (Royal Regiment of Fusiliers); Major Smiley (Grenadier Guards); Miss Rose Talbot; Major Wemyss (Royal Green Jackets); Sir Ronald Wingate, Bart. Lt Colonel Uloth, British Military Attaché in Khartoum, has in particular been lavish in help and encouragement.

Bibliography

The River War by Winston Churchill (London, Vol I 1899, Vol II 1900) is by far the best account of the whole campaign. Other books covering all or part of it are:

The Egyptian Soudan. Its Loss and Recovery, H. S. Alford and W. Dennistoun Sword, London 1898
The Downfall of the Dervishes, Ernest Bennett, London 1898
Khartoum Campaign, Bennet Burleigh, London 1899
The Egyptian Campaigns, Charles Royle, London 1900
With Kitchener to Khartoum, G. W. Steevens, London 1898

With Kitchener's Army, Owen Spencer Watkins, London 1899
Sudan Campaign, By 'An Officer', London 1899

It would be pointless to cite all the regimental histories which have some reference to Omdurman but churlish not to acknowledge the especial value of *The Royal Engineers in Egypt and the Sudan* by Lt Colonel Sandes (Chatham 1937), one of the best books of the kind that can ever have been written.

Among the many biographies and autobiographies on which I have drawn, I would particularly like to pay tribute to Sir Philip Magnus's impressive and brilliantly entertaining life of Kitchener (*Portrait of an Imperialist*. London 1958) and Mr Gordon Brook-Shepherd's excellent new biography of Slatin Pasha, *Between Two Flags*, London 1973.

I should also mention:

Service Through Six Reigns, A.F.C. (Privately Printed 1953)
The Life and Letters of David Beatty, W. S. Chalmers, London 1951
Memoirs, Babikr Bedri, Oxford 1972
Winston S. Churchill, Youth, 1874–1900, Randolph Churchill, London
    1966 (with companion volume of documents)
Haig, Duff Cooper, London 1935
Douglas Haig, John Terraine, London 1963
High Pressure, Lt Colonel Lionel James, London 1929
Hector Macdonald, Thomas Coates, London 1900
Toll for the Brave, John Montgomery, London 1963
Life of General Lord Rawlinson, F. Maurice, London 1928
Vestigia, Lt Colonel Charles à Court Repington, London 1919
A Sheaf of Memories, Frank·Scudamore, London 1925
Memories of Forty-Eight Years Service, Horace Smith-Dorrien, London
    1925
Townshend of Kut, A. J. Barker, London 1967
Seymour Vandeleur, Colonel F. Maxse, London 1905
Peaceful Personalities and Warriors Bold, Fred Villiers, London 1907
Major General Wauchope, Sir George Douglas, London 1904
Wingate of the Sudan, Ronald Wingate, London 1955

Of especial interest for the background to the campaign I have found:

The Mahdist State in the Sudan, P. M. Holt, Oxford 1958
A Prisoner of the Khaleefa, Charles Neufeld, London 1899
Ten Years' Captivity in the Mahdi's Camp, Father Ohrwalder, London
    1893
Fire and Sword in the Sudan, Rudolf Slatin, London 1896

All other material has been drawn from articles published in military journals or from letters and diaries in regimental museums or private collections.

List of Illustrations

Page numbers in bold type indicate illustrations in colour

cers at the Battle of Omdurman. Painting by R. Caton Woodville. *The Walker Art Gallery, Liverpool.*

154. Colonel Martin leading the charge of the 21st Lancers. *Photo Radio Times Hulton Picture Library.*

157. Lieut. the Hon. de Montmorency and his Sergeant-Major after the charge of the 21st Lancers. *17th/21st Lancers Regimental Museum, Belvoir Castle, Grantham. Photo Eileen Tweedy.*

169. Colonel Macdonald's brigade repelling an attack. *Photo Radio Times Hulton Picture Library.*

177. The fight for the Khalifa's black flag. *Photo Radio Times Hulton Picture Library.*

181. The Flight of the Khalifa. Detail from a painting by R. Talbot Kelly. *The Walker Art Gallery, Liverpool.*

182. Sudanese looting after the battle. *Photo National Army Museum.*

189. Kitchener leaving the battlefield with his own flag and the Khalifa's black banner in the rear. *Royal Commonwealth Society Library. Photo Eileen Tweedy.*

191. Kitchener's entry into Omdur-man. *Illustrated London News. Photo Eileen Tweedy.*

192. The Heavy Camel Corps. *Guards Museum, Wellington Barracks. Photo Eileen Tweedy.*

198. Lt.-Col. J. G. Maxwell leading his brigade into Omdurman. *17th/21st Lancers Regimental Museum, Belvoir Castle, Grantham. Photo Eileen Tweedy.*

206. Neufeld with his native wife and children. *Guards Museum, Wellington Barracks. Photo Eileen Tweedy.*

207. Neufeld in his German attaché's clothes. *Guards Museum, Wellington Barracks. Photo Eileen Tweedy.*

218/219. Gordon Memorial Service, Khartoum, 1898. Painting by R. Caton Woodville. *Reproduced by Gracious Permission of Her Majesty the Queen.*

225. Assembled troops sing the National Anthem as flags are raised in Omdurman. *Guards Museum, Wellington Barracks. Photo Eileen Tweedy.*

230. The dead body of the Khalifa, November 1899. *Photo Radio Times Hulton Picture Library.*

232. Chief tomb of the Dervishes at Kerreri. *Photo National Army Museum.*

MAPS

237

Index

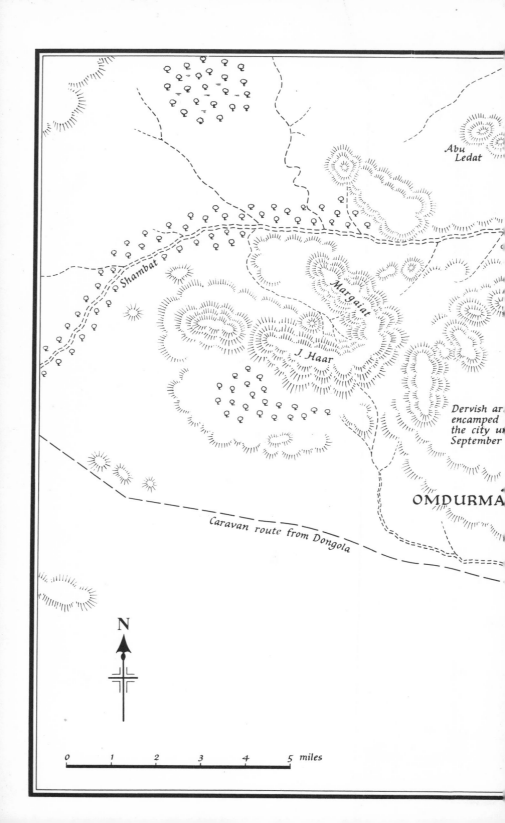

Abu
Ledat

Shambat

Margaiat

J. Haar

Dervish ar
encamped
the city u
September

OMDURMA

Caravan route from Dongola

N

0   1   2   3   4   5 miles